WORLD ENGLISH Intro

Real People • Real Places • Real Language

Martin Milner

HEINLE
CENGAGE Learning™

Australia • Brazil • Japan • Korea • Mexico • Singapore • Spain • United Kingdom • United States

World English Intro
Real People • Real Places • Real Language
Martin Milner

Publisher: Sherrise Roehr

Managing Editor: Berta de Llano

Senior Development Editor: Margarita Matte

Development Editor: Michael Poor

National Geographic Editorial Liaison:
 Leila Hishmeh

Technology Development Manager:
 Debie Mirtle

Director of Global Marketing: Ian Martin

Director of US Marketing: Jim McDonough

Product Marketing Manager: Katie Kelley

Marketing Assistant: Jide Iruka

Senior Content Project Manager/Art Direction:
 Dawn Marie Elwell

Senior Print Buyer: Betsy Donaghey

For permission to use material from this text or product,
submit all requests online at **cengage.com/permissions**
Further permissions questions can be emailed to
permissionrequest@cengage.com

Library of Congress Control Number: 2008937885

International Edition:
World English Intro ISBN 13: 978-1-4240-5014-7
World English Intro ISBN 10: 1-4240-5014-6
World English Intro + CD-ROM ISBN 13: 978-1-4240-3476-5
World English Intro + CD-ROM ISBN 10: 1-4240-3476-0

U.S. Edition:
World English Intro ISBN 13: 978-1-4240-6335-2
World English Intro ISBN 10: 1-4240-6335-3

Heinle
20 Channel Center Street
Boston, MA 02210
USA

Cengage Learning is a leading provider of customized learning solutions with office locations around the globe, including Singapore, the United Kingdom, Australia, Mexico, Brazil, and Japan. Locate your local office at:
international.cengage.com/region

Cengage Learning products are represented in Canada by Nelson Education, Ltd.

Visit Heinle online at elt.heinle.com

Visit our corporate website at www.cengage.com

Printed in Canada
1 2 3 4 5 6 7 13 12 11 10 09

CONTENTS

	Unit Goals	Grammar	Vocabulary	Listening	Speaking and Pronunciation	Reading and Writing
UNIT 1	**Friends and Family** page 2					
	• Meet and introduce people • Identify family members • Describe people • Give personal and family information	Simple present tense: *Be* *I'm Kim.* *They're Maria and Lola.* *Be* + adjective *They're young.* *Is John single?*	Greetings and introductions Family members Adjectives	Listening for general understanding and specific information	Talking about your family tree */r/* sound	"Families around the World" Writing sentences to describe people
UNIT 2	**Jobs Around the World** page 14					
	• Identify jobs • Talk about jobs • Talk about countries • Compare jobs in different countries	*Be*: Negative *He isn't a doctor.* Indefinite article *Pat's an artist.* *Be* + article + adjective + noun *Russia is a big country.*	Jobs Numbers Continents, countries, and cities	Focused listening People describing their jobs	Asking for and giving personal information Contractions with *be*	"Different Farmers" Writing a paragraph to describe a person's job
UNIT 3	**Houses and Apartments** page 26					
	• Identify rooms in a house • Describe your house • Identify household objects • Compare houses	*There is/there are* *There are three bedrooms.* *Is there a garage?* Prepositions of place: *in, on, under, next to* *Your magazine is under your bag.*	Rooms in a house Furniture and household objects	Listening for general understanding and specific details People talking about their houses	Describing your house Final *–s*	"Unusual Houses" Writing descriptions of houses
UNIT 4	**Possessions** page 38					
	• Identify personal possessions • Talk about personal possessions • Buy a present • Talk about special possessions	Demonstrative adjectives *Are these your books?* *That is not your bag.* Possessive nouns *It's Jim's bag.* *Have* *She has a camcorder.*	Personal possessions Electronic products	Listening for specific information People proving ownership	Talking about the personal possessions of others Differentiating short *i* and long *e* sounds	"Jewelry" Summarizing a class survey
UNIT 5	**Daily Activities** page 50					
	• Tell time • Ask about people's daily activities • Talk about what you do at work • Describe a job	Simple present tense: statements, negatives, questions, and short answers *They get up at 7 o'clock.* *What time do you start work?* Adverbs of frequency: *always, sometimes, never* *I never answer the phone.*	Daily activities Telling time Professional activities	Listening for general understanding and specific details Describing a photographer's work	Asking and answering questions about work activities Falling intonation on statements and information questions	"Robots at Work" Writing a job description
UNIT 6	**Getting There** page 62					
	• Ask for and give directions • Create and use a tour route • Talk about transportation • Record a journey	Imperatives *Turn left and walk for two blocks.* *Have to* *She has to change buses.*	City landmarks Directions Ground Transportation	Listening for specific information Radio ad for a tour	Ask for and give directions *Yes/no* questions	"Shackleton's Epic Journey" Writing a travel journal

	Unit Goals	Grammar	Vocabulary	Listening	Speaking and Pronunciation	Reading and Writing
UNIT 7	**Free Time** page 74 • Identify activities that are happening now • Talk about activities that are happening now • Talk about abilities • Talk about sports	Present continuous tense *I'm not watching television. I'm reading.* *Can* (for ability) *He **can't** play the guitar.* *He **can** sing.*	Pastimes Games and sports	Listening for specific information Telephone conversation	Have a phone conversation *sh* and *ch* sounds	"Sports—Then and Now" Writing sentences about your abilities
UNIT 8	**Clothes** page 86 • Identify and buy clothes • Say what people are wearing • Express likes and dislikes • Learn about clothes and colors	*Can/could* (for polite requests) ***Can** I try on these shoes?* Likes and dislikes *I **love** your sweater!* *She **can't stand** pink.*	Clothes Colors	Listening for specific details	Describing people's clothes *Could you*	"Chameleon Clothes" Writing about what people are wearing
UNIT 9	**Eat Well** page 98 • Order a meal • Plan a party • Talk about a healthy diet • Talk about food for special occasions	*Some, any* *There's **some** ice cream in the fridge.* *How much/ how many* ***How many** oranges do we need?* ***How much** chocolate do we have?*	Food types Meals Count/non-count nouns	Listening for specific details Conversation to confirm a shopping list	Planning a dinner *And*	"Special Days, Special Food" Writing sentences to summarize information
UNIT 10	**Health** page 110 • Identify parts of the body to say how you feel • Ask about and describe symptoms • Identify remedies and give advice • Learn and talk about prevention	Review of simple present tense *Look* + adjective *Feel* + adjective *John **looks** terrible.* *I **feel** sick.* *My back **hurts**.* *Should* (for advice) *You **should** take an aspirin.*	Parts of the body Common illnesses Remedies	Listening for general understanding and specific details Doctor's appointments	Describing symptoms and illnesses; giving advice Word stress	"Preventing Disease" Writing a notice board
UNIT 11	**Making Plans** page 122 • Plan special days • Plan holidays • Make life plans • Express wishes and plans	*Be going to* *What **are** you **going to** do?* *We **are going to** have a party.* *Would like* (for wishes) *I **would like** to be a doctor.*	Special plans American holidays Professions	Listening for general understanding and specific details	Talking about celebrating holidays Reduced *Be going to*	"Life's Milestones" Writing about one's plans for the future
UNIT 12	**Migrations** page 134 • Talk about moving in the past • Talk about moving dates • Talk about preparations for moving • Discuss migrations	Simple past tense *We **went** to the mountains.* *He **moved** from San Francisco to New York.*	Verbs + prepositions of movement Travel preparations	Listening for general understanding and specific details Biographies of famous immigrants	Discussing moving *–ed* sounds	"Human Migration" Writing a vacation postcard

Nunavut, Canada
Find out how people dress to keep warm in the Arctic. *Inuit Fashion*

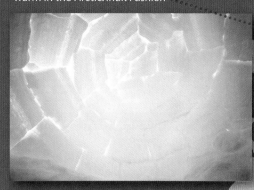

San Francisco, California, United States of America
What other work do dentists do? *Zoo Dentists*

Michoacan, Mexico
Millions of monarch butterflies travel more than 2000 miles every year. *Monarch Migration*

Heimaey, Iceland
Are children good workers? Learn about the puffin rescuers in Iceland. *A Job for Children*

Your World!

Camogli, Italy
See how people decorate their houses in this fishing village. *A Very Special Village*

Greve in Chianti, Italy
Do we eat too fast? Learn about the Slow Food Movement. *Slow Food*

Chiang Mai, Thailand
Why does a 12-year old boy want to become a boxing champion? *Making a Thai Boxing Champion*

Afar, Ethiopia
How do geologists learn about volcanoes? Watch a close-up expedition. *Volcano Trek*

Vanuatu
Do you think bungee jumping is dangerous? Watch boys and men jump from a high tower and hit the ground! *Land Divers of Vanuatu*

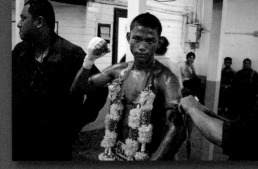

Nairobi, Kenya
Can a small white flower save lives? Yes. The pyrethrum kills the mosquito that spreads malaria. *Pyrethrum*

= Sites of the video clips you will view in *World English Intro*.

FRIENDS AND

1. Are these people friends or family?

2. Are these people young or old?

UNIT GOALS

Meet and introduce people
Identify family members
Describe people
Give personal and family information

FAMILY

Vocabulary

A. Listen and repeat.

Track 1-2   **Greetings**

Informal	Formal
Hi! How's it going?	Fine, thank you. And how are you?
Great! And you?	Good morning. How are you?
Fine. OK. So-so.	Good afternoon. Good evening.

B. Greet your classmates informally.

C. Greet your teacher formally.

D. Listen and repeat.

Track 1-3   **Introductions**

Introducing yourself	Introducing another person
Hi, I'm Elsa.	This is my friend Hussein.
Hello, pleased to meet you. I'm Alan.	Nice to meet you too.
	Nice to meet you, Hussein.
My name's Alan.	Do you know Hussein?

E. Introduce yourself to your classmates.

F. Work in groups of three. Practice introducing each other.

Grammar: Present tense *be*

Subject pronoun	*Be*	
I	am	
You	are	Kim.
He/She	is	
We	are	Ron and Ed.
They	are	Maria and Claudia.

Contractions with *be*

I'm
You're
He's
She's
We're
They're

A. Unscramble the sentences.

1. Ron.　name　My　is <u>My name is Ron.</u>
2. Leila.　is　name　Her _____
3. is　name　Mr. Aoki.　His_____
4. Tim.　Their　Jan　names　are　and _____
5. name　Your　is　Yan-Ching. _____

Possessive adjectives

My	name is Mario.
Your	name is Rachel.
His	name is Robert.
Her	name is Liujun.
Their	names are Ben and Dan.

B. Write the sentences again. Use contractions.

1. He is Ruben.　<u>He's Ruben.</u>
2. I am Peter. _____
3. You are Rebecca. _____
4. They are Ashley and Jason. _____
5. We are Carol and Melissa. _____

Conversation

A. Listen to the conversation. Spell Hiroshi.

 Track 1-5

Donna:	Hi, Nick. How are you?
Nick:	Great. And you?
Donna:	Fine.
Nick:	Donna, this is my friend Hiroshi.
Donna:	Nice to meet you, Hir . . . sorry?
Hiroshi:	It's Hiroshi. H-I-R-O-S-H-I. Nice to meet you, Donna.

Track 1-4

Word Focus

The English alphabet =
A B C D E F G H I J K L
M N O P Q R S T U V W
X Y Z

Real Language

We sometimes spell
our names for people.

 B. Practice the conversation in groups of three. Switch roles and practice it again.

 C. Practice the conversation again. Use your own names.

Goal 1　Meet and introduce people

Work in pairs. Find another pair and introduce each other.

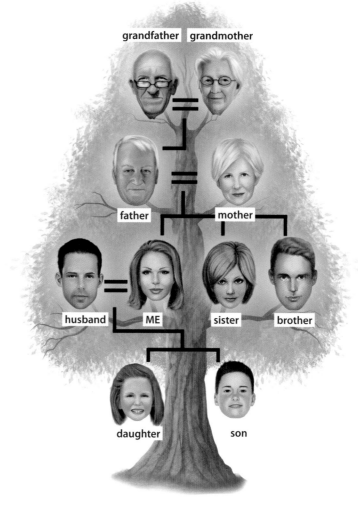

grandfather | grandmother

father | mother

husband | ME | sister | brother

daughter | son

Listening

A. Listen to Carlos introduce his family. Point to the people and pets.

Track 1-6

B. Listen again. Circle **T** for *true* and **F** for *false*.

Track 1-6

Carlos says:

1. This is my grandfather. His name is Pedro.   (T)   F
2. This is my sister. Her name is Karina.   T   F
3. This is my grandmother. Her name is Elena.   T   F
4. This is my father. His name is Jose Manuel.   T   F
5. These are our dogs. Their names are Lucy and Lulu. T   F

C. Correct any *false* sentences. Take turns to read all the sentences to a partner.

D. Fill in the blanks in Carlos's family tree.

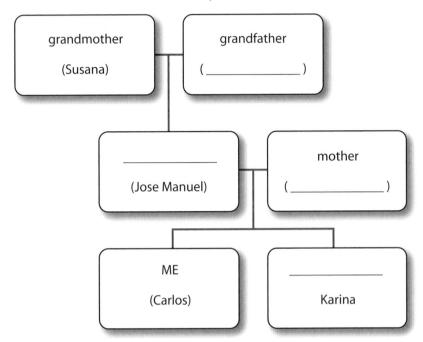

grandmother
(Susana)

grandfather
(_____)

_____
(Jose Manuel)

mother
(_____)

ME
(Carlos)

_____
Karina

Pronunciation: The /r/ sound

Track 1-7

A. <u>Underline</u> the letter *r*. Listen to the /r/ sound and repeat the word.

father	Rick
mother	Rose
sister	Robert Brown
brother	Mary Brown

 B. Take turns reading the words to a partner.

Communication

A. Draw your own family tree.

 B. Describe the family tree to a partner.

✓ **Goal 2** **Identify family members**

This is my grandmother. Her name is Aiko.

Bring some family photos to class. Introduce your family to your classmates.

Language Expansion: Adjectives

tall	young	married	handsome
short	old	single	pretty

1.

2.

3.

4.

curly	straight	wavy	straight	curly
black hair	gray hair	red hair	blond hair	brown hair

A. Write adjectives to describe these people.

1. They are _____. He is _____. She is _____.
2. He is _____ with _____ hair.
3. She is _____ with _____ hair.
4. They are _____ with _____ hair.

B. Now describe yourself.
I am _____ with _____ hair.

Grammar: *Be* + adjective

Subject	*Be*	Adjective
I	am	young.
You	are	tall.
John	is	single.
Emily	is	pretty.
We	are	married.
They	are	old.

Questions with *be* and short answers

Questions			Short answers	
Are	you	married?	Yes, I am.	No, I'm not.
Is	he/she	single?	Yes, he/she is.	No, he/she isn't.
Are	they	married?	Yes, they are.	No, they're not.

A. Match the questions and the answers.

Questions
1. Is your brother tall? _b_
2. Are your brothers married? ____
3. Is Emma pretty? ____
4. Is your brother single? ____
5. Are your mother and father old? ____

Answers
a. Yes, she is.
b. No, he isn't. He's short.
c. Alan is married. Brian isn't.
d. No, they're not.
e. No, he isn't. He's married.

B. Write the questions.

1. Q: _____?
   A: No, she isn't. She's tall.
2. Q: _____?
   A: **Yes, they are.**
3. Q: _____?
   A: **Yes, I** am.

Conversation

Track 1-8

A. Look at the pictures and listen to the conversation.

Ana: Who's this?
Carol: It's my <u>brother</u>.
Ana: What's his name?
Carol: <u>Richard.</u>
Ana: Is he married?
Carol: Yes, he is.
Ana: What a shame!

B. Practice the conversation with a partner. Switch roles and practice it again.

C. Change the underlined words and make a new conversation.

✓ **Goal 3**   **Describe people**

Work with a partner. Take turns describing your classmates.

Reading

A. Look at the pictures. Show a partner where these people are from on the map.

B. Complete the sentences with words from the box.

| mother blond son married black |

1. June Banks is the _____ of Kevin and Kate.
2. Ian Banks has curly _____ hair.
3. Bo is the _____ of Feng and Huan.
4. Mrs. Patel has _____ hair.
5. Alisha is _____ to Ramesh.

C. Circle the correct answers.

1. Her father is Ian Banks.
   a. June
   b. Kate
2. They live in Scotland.
   a. Kevin and Kate
   b. Feng and Huan
3. His wife is Huan.
   a. Feng
   b. Bo
4. Her daughters are Alisha and Rasha.
   a. Mrs. Patel
   b. Suchir
5. Her husband is Ramesh.
   a. Alisha
   b. Rasha

Families around the World

This is the Banks family. They come from Scotland. Ian is tall with curly blond hair. His wife, June, has wavy brown hair. Ian and June have two children: a son and a young daughter. Their names are Kevin and Kate.

Meet Feng and his family. They are from China. His wife's name is Huan. They have one son. His name is Bo. He is young. He is two years old.

This is the Patel family. They are from India. Mrs. Patel has two daughters. They are married. Their names are Alisha and Rasha. Their husbands are Ramesh and Suchir. Alisha is married to Ramesh. Rasha is married to Suchir. They all have black hair.

Communication

Look at the photos. Choose one photo. Describe a person to a partner. Your partner guesses who you are describing.

He is tall with curly blond hair. He is young and handsome.

Is it David?

Yes, it is!

1. David

2. Ayako

3. Alonso

4. Michelle

Writing

Write a description of a family member.

He is tall with curly black hair. He is single.

✓ **Goal 4** **Give personal and family information**

Work with a partner. Take turns describing your family.

Before You Watch

Label the animals. Use the words in the box.

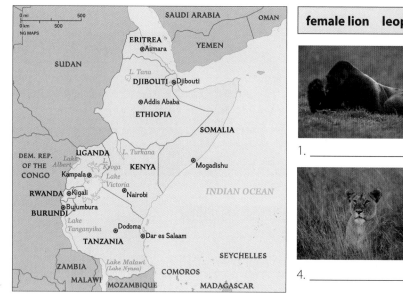

▲ East Africa

| female lion | leopard | male gorilla | meerkats | male lion | polar bear |

1. _____ 2. _____ 3. _____

4. _____ 5. _____ 6. _____

While You Watch

A. Watch the video. Circle **T** for *true* and **F** for *false*.

1. Polar bears have big families.   T F
2. Lions live in family groups.   T F
3. Male lions have red hair.   T F
4. Meerkats are big.   T F
5. Female gorillas have gray hair on their backs.   T F

B. Complete the sentences. Use the words in the box.

pretty	big	long	lions	male

1. There is one male in a family of _____.
2. A male lion has _____ hair on his neck.
3. Meerkats live in _____ groups.
4. Young meerkats are _____.
5. The _____ gorilla is the leader of the family.

 C. Watch the video to check your answers.

After You Watch

▲ a rhino   ▲ a dolphin   ▲ an ant   ▲ a sloth   ▲ a wolf

A. Write the names of the animals in the correct box.

	Big	**Small**
Live in groups	lions	meerkats
Live alone	polar bears	

B. Compare your answers with a partner's answers.

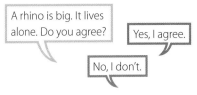

A rhino is big. It lives alone. Do you agree?

Yes, I agree.

No, I don't.

1. Where are these people from?

2. What are their jobs?

UNIT GOALS

Identify jobs
Talk about jobs
Talk about countries
Compare jobs in different countries

Vocabulary

🎧 **A.** What do they do? Listen and label the pictures with words from the box.

Track 1-9

taxi driver	chef	engineer	teacher
banker	architect	doctor	artist

1. Oscar _____   2. Eun _____   3. Jane _____   4. Dae-Jung _____

5. Jim _____   6. Hannah _____   7. Harvey _____   8. Fernanda _____

B. In your opinion, are these jobs interesting or boring? Write the jobs from exercise **A** on the lines.

boring ← ⊢⊢⊢⊢⊢⊢⊢⊢⊢⊢ → interesting

👥 **C.** Compare your answers with a partner's answers.

Grammar: *Be* (negative)

Be + not			
I	am		a doctor.
You	are	**not**	
He/she	is		
We/they	are		doctors.

Contractions	
I'm not	you aren't
you're not	he/she isn't
he's not/she's not	we aren't
we're not	they aren't
they're not	

Indefinite article

Jim's **a** doctor.
Pat's **an** artist.

*We use **a** before a consonant sound.
*We use **an** before a vowel sound.

A. Look at the pictures on the opposite page. Fill in the blanks with *is* or *is not*.

1. Jim _____is_____ a taxi driver. He _____is not_____ a doctor.
2. Oscar _____ a teacher. He _____ an architect.
3. Fernanda _____ an architect. She _____ a doctor.
4. Dae-Jung _____ an engineer. He _____ a chef.
5. Eun _____ a banker. She _____ an artist.

B. Circle **T** for *true* and **F** for *false*.

1. Hannah is a taxi driver.	T	Ⓕ
2. Jane is an engineer.	T	F
3. Dae-Jung is an artist.	T	F
4. Eun is not an artist.	T	F
5. Harvey is not an architect.	T	F

 **C.** Correct the false sentences. Read the new sentences to a partner.

> Hannah isn't a taxi driver. She is a doctor.

Conversation

 A. Listen to the conversation. Is Jill married or single?

Track 1-10

Mary: Hi, Jean. How's life?
Jean: Fine. And you?
Mary: Great. How are the children?
Jean: They're good. But they're not children now. Jim's married. He's <u>an engineer</u>.
Mary: <u>Wow</u>! Time passes. And what about Jill? How old is she now?
Jean: She's <u>21</u> and she's <u>a student</u>.
Mary: Is she married?
Jean: No, she's still single.

 B. Practice the conversation with a partner. Switch roles and practice it again.

 C. Change the underlined words and make a new conversation.

Real Language

To show surprise, we can say:

formal ◄────────► informal
Really!   Amazing!   Wow!

> What do you do?

> What does your father do?

✓ Goal 1   Identify jobs

Ask your classmates about their jobs. Ask them about their family's jobs.

Listening

 Track 1-11

A. Look at the pictures. Guess the people's jobs. Listen and check your guesses.

▲ Michelle ▲ Carlos ▲ Salim

 Track 1-11

B. Listen again. Fill in the blanks in the chart.

	Michelle	**Carlos**	**Salim**
How old is he/she?			
What is his/her job?			
Is his/her job interesting?			

C. Work with a partner. Take turns reading the numbers in English.

Real Language

To ask about someone's age, we say: *How old is he/she?* The answer is: *She's/He's 28 years old.*

Numbers	**10** ten	**20** twenty	**30** thirty
1 one	**11** eleven	**21** twenty-one	**40** forty
2 two	**12** twelve	**22** twenty-two	**50** fifty
3 three	**13** thirteen	**23** twenty-three	**60** sixty
4 four	**14** fourteen	**24** twenty-four	**70** seventy
5 five	**15** fifteen	**25** twenty-five	**80** eighty
6 six	**16** sixteen	**26** twenty-six	**90** ninety
7 seven	**17** seventeen	**27** twenty-seven	**100** one hundred
8 eight	**18** eighteen	**28** twenty-eight	**101** one hundred and
9 nine	**19** nineteen	**29** twenty-nine	one

D. Now tell a partner about the people in exercise **B**.

Pronunciation: Contractions with *be*

A. Listen and circle what you hear.

Track 1-12

1.	(I am)	I'm	
2.	I am not	I'm not	
3.	you are	you're	
4.	you are not	you aren't	you're not
5.	she is	she's	
6.	she is not	she isn't	she's not
7.	we are	we're	
8.	we are not	we're not	we aren't
9.	they are	they're	
10.	they are not	they're not	they aren't

B. Take turns reading the phrases in exercise **A**. Point to the phrases as a partner reads them.

Communication

Read the questions and answer them for yourself. Then ask two classmates the questions. Write their answers.

Questions	Me	Classmate 1	Classmate 2
What is your name?			
What is your job?			
Is it interesting?			

Ivan is 27 years old and he's a computer technician.

His job is interesting.

✓ Goal 2 Talk about jobs

Tell a partner about the people you interviewed.

Language Expansion: Countries and Cities

▲ wet   ▲ hot   ▲ cold   ▲ dry

Guess the country.

1. It's in Asia. It's big. It's cold. ___China___
2. It's in Europe. It's small. It's wet. _____
3. It's in South America. It's big. It's hot. _____
4. It's in South America. It's small. The capital is Santiago. _____
5. It's in North America. It's hot. _____

Grammar: *Be* + adjective + noun

Statement	Question	Answer
Africa is a big continent.	Is the United Kingdom (UK) a big country?	No, it isn't. It's a small country.
Egypt is a hot, dry country.	Is the United States a big country?	Yes, it is.

Word Focus

We say **the** *United Kingdom* and **the** *United States*.

A. Unscramble the sentences.

1. China Is a country? big _____
2. big The is a country. United States _____
3. is a Russia country. cold _____
4. Is hot Egypt a country? _____
5. country. small Japan is a _____

B. Answer the questions.

1. Is Mexico a cold country?   No, it isn't. It's a hot country.
2. Is Chile a big country? _____
3. Is Japan a hot country? _____
4. Is the UK a small country? _____
5. Is Egypt a wet country? _____

Conversation

Track 1-13

A. Listen to the conversation. Where is Mohamed from?

Alan:	Where do you come from, <u>Mohamed</u>?
Mohamed:	I'm from <u>Cairo</u>.
Alan:	<u>Cairo</u> is in <u>Egypt</u>, right?
Mohamed:	Yes.
Alan:	So, tell me about <u>Egypt, Mohamed</u>.
Mohamed:	Well, it's in <u>Africa—North Africa</u>.
Alan:	Is it a <u>hot</u> country?
Mohamed:	Yes, it's <u>very hot</u>.

B. Practice the conversation with a partner. Switch roles and practice it again.

C. Change the underlined words and make a new conversation.

✔ **Goal 3**   **Talk about countries**

Talk to a partner. Describe some countries in your region of the world.

Reading

A. Look at the pictures. Describe the people to a partner.

B. Complete the sentences. Use the words in the box.

grapes	millet and maize	Chile
farmer	Europe	Africa
brothers		

1. Elena is from _____.
2. She is a _____.
3. She grows _____.
4. Her wine goes to _____.
5. Solomon and Abraham are from
   _____.
6. They grow _____.
7. They are _____.

C. Answer the questions.

1. Is it wet in Chile in the summer?

   _____

2. Is Elena's wine good?

   _____

3. Are Solomon and Abraham brothers?

   _____

4. Are they good farmers?

   _____

5. Is it cold in Namibia?

   _____

The Southern Hemisphere

Different Farmers

Elena is from Chile, and she is a farmer. She grows grapes and makes wine. The weather in Chile is good for grapes. In summer it is hot and dry, and in winter it is cold and wet. Her wine is very good. It goes to North America and Europe.

CHILE

▲ maize

▲ millet

NAMIBIA

Solomon and Abraham are brothers. They are from Namibia in Africa. They are farmers. They grow millet and maize for their family. The weather in Namibia is good for millet. It is hot and dry. Solomon and Abraham are good farmers.

Communication

Look at the pictures. Discuss the following questions with a partner.

1. Where are these people from?
2. What do they do?
3. Are they old or young?
4. Are their jobs interesting?

▲ Aastik

▲ Henry

Writing

Read about Aastik.

> Aastik is from Nepal. He is a farmer but his farm is very small. He grows rice. His rice does not go to other countries. It is for his family.

Write a similar paragraph about Henry. Use these words: United States, big, wheat, Asia.

_____

_____

_____

✔ **Goal 4** **Compare jobs in different countries**

Talk to a partner about farmers in your country. What do they grow? What is the weather like? Are their jobs interesting or boring?

sky

cliffs

sea

beach

box

▲ a puffin

Before You Watch

Work with a partner. Look at the picture. Answer these questions.

1. What do these children do?
2. Are they old or young?
3. Is their job interesting?

While You Watch

A. Watch the video. Label the pictures below.

> **Puffin patrols look for lost puffins.**
> **Puffins get lost.**
> **Children find lost puffins.**
> **Puffins leave the cliffs.**

Word Focus

exciting=
interesting, fun
crash into=
run into; hit

B. Watch the video again. Circle **T** for *true* and **F** for *false*.

1. Puffin patrols look for bird nests.   T   F
2. There are puffin nests in the cliffs.   T   F
3. All the puffins fly out to sea.   T   F
4. Some puffins get lost in town.   T   F
5. Puffin patrols rescue pufflings.   T   F

C. Complete the sentences with the words or phrases in the box. Watch the video again to check your answers.

look for   rescue   leave   throw   get lost

1. Some puffins _____ in town.
2. The pufflings _____ the cliffs.
3. The children _____ the pufflings out to sea.
4. The puffin patrols _____ the lost pufflings in parking lots.
5. The children's job is to _____ the puffins.

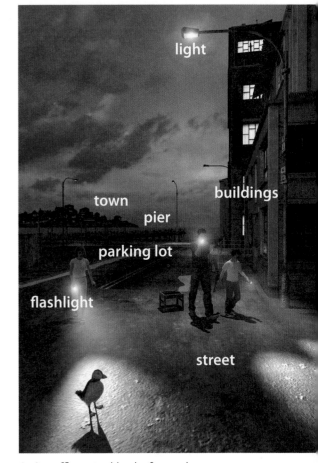

▲ A puffin patrol looks for and rescues lost pufflings.

After You Watch

Work with a partner. Take turns describing the job of the puffin patrols.

Word Focus

ALL PUFFINS   some puffins

HOUSES AND

1. Where are these houses?

2. Are these houses like your house?

UNIT GOALS

Identify rooms in a house
Describe your house
Identify household objects
Compare houses

Vocabulary

A. Label the rooms in the apartment.

1. _____
2. _____
5. _____
3. _____
4. _____

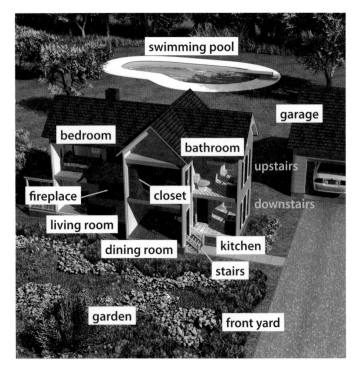

B. Complete the sentences about the house in the picture. Use the words in the box.

garage	downstairs	living room	fireplace	bedrooms

1. The kitchen is _____.
2. The _____ is in the backyard.
3. The _____ are upstairs.
4. The _____ is in the _____.

Grammar: *There is/there are*

Statement	Questions	Answers
There is a garage.	**Is there** a closet?	Yes, there is. No, there isn't.
There are three bedrooms upstairs.	**Are there** two bathrooms?	Yes, there are. No, there aren't.

*The contraction of *there is* = *there's*.

Plural nouns

1 house	2 houses
1 bedroom	2 bedrooms

*Add an -s at the end of the word to make it plural.

A. Complete the sentences with the correct form: *there is* or *there are*.

1. _____ a big kitchen.
2. _____ three bathrooms.
3. _____ a yard?
4. Is there a closet? Yes, _____.
5. Is there a garage? No, _____.

B. Unscramble the sentences.

1. a   is   big   There   garage _____.
2. isn't   There   closet   a _____.
3. a   swimming   Is   there   pool _____?
4. there   two   Are   bathrooms _____?
5. garages   are   There   two _____.

Conversation

Track 1-14

A. Listen to the conversation. Is there a garage?

Realtor: What about this <u>apartment</u>?
Client: Is it a big apartment?
Realtor: Yes, there are <u>three bedrooms</u>.
Client: And <u>bathrooms</u>?
Realtor: There is just one bathroom.
Client: Is there a <u>garden</u>?
Realtor: No, there isn't. But there's a garage.

Luxury Apartment — 1st floor

- Big kitchen/ dining room
- Living room
- 3 bedrooms
- 1 bathroom

 B. Practice the conversation with a partner. Switch roles and practice it again.

 C. Change the underlined words and make a new conversation.

Real Language

What about is a useful and simple way to ask for someone's opinion.

 Goal 1   Identify rooms in a house

Work with a partner. Draw a simple floor plan like the apartment on page 28. Tell your partner the names of the rooms.

Listening

🎧
Track 1-15

A. Listen to each person describe his or her house. Match the names to the pictures.

| Betty Joe Katsuro Ramon Liling |

1. _____

2. _____

3. _____

4. _____

5. _____

B. Listen again. Circle **T** for *true* and **F** for *false*.

1. There is one bedroom in Betty's house.   T   F
2. There are four bedrooms in Joe's house.   T   F
3. There is a fireplace in Katsuro's house.   T   F
4. There are five bedrooms in Ramon's house.   T   F
5. There is a yard in Liling's house.   T   F

Pronunciation: *Final -s*

Track 1-16

A. Listen and check the correct column.

	Ends in /s/ sound	Ends in /z/ sound	Ends in /iz/ sound
gardens			
apartments			
garages			
bathrooms			
kitchens			
houses			
windows			

Track 1-16

B. Listen again and repeat the words.

Communication

Work with a partner. Take turns describing these houses.

There is one bedroom in this house.

Goal 2   **Describe your house**

Describe your house to the class.

Language Expansion: Furniture and household objects

▲ sofa   ▲ bed   ▲ armchair   ▲ refrigerator

▲ table   ▲ chair   ▲ bookcase   ▲ microwave

▲ coffee table   ▲ lamp   ▲ stove   ▲TV

In which rooms do you usually find the furniture and household objects above?

Kitchen	Dining room	Living room	Bedroom
stove			

Grammar: Prepositions of place

▲ in   ▲ on   ▲ under   ▲ next to

A. Look at the pictures. Complete the sentences with *in*, *on*, *under*, or *next to*.

1. There's a TV _____ the bedroom.
2. There's a boy _____ the swimming pool.
3. There are three books _____ the table.
4. The stove is _____ the refrigerator.
5. The dog is _____ the table.

B. What can you see in the pictures? Take turns describing them.

> There is a sofa and a coffee table.

Conversation

A. Listen to the conversation. Where is Tracey's magazine?

Track 1-17

Tracey: Where is my <u>magazine</u>?
Kevin: Is it in the <u>bedroom</u>?
Tracey: No, it isn't. And it's not on the <u>kitchen table</u>.
Kevin: Here it is! It's under your <u>bag</u>.

B. Practice the conversation with a partner. Switch roles and practice it again.

C. Change the underlined words and make a new conversation.

 Goal 3   **Identify household objects**

Work with a partner. Take turns describing a room in your house.

Reading

A. Look at the pictures. Where do you think the houses are?

B. Read and answer the questions.

1. Is there a bathroom in the tree house? _____

2. Is it hot in an igloo? _____

3. How many rooms are in the igloo? _____

4. Are there a lot of rooms in Dar Al Hajar? _____

5. Are there bedrooms in the Crooked House? _____

▲ an Irian Jaya treehouse

Unusual Houses

The Kombai people of Irian Jaya live in tree houses. The houses are high in the trees. There is only one room in the house. It is the kitchen, the living room, the dining room, and the bedroom.

Abraham Niaqu is from Quebec in Canada. He is making a snow house called an *igloo*. There is only one room in an igloo. It is not cold in an igloo. In fact, it is quite hot.

This house is called Dar Al Hajar. It is in Yemen. It is a big house and there are a lot of rooms in the house. It is hot in Yemen, but it is not hot inside the house.

This house is called the Crooked House. However, it is not a house. Nobody lives in it. It is a shop—a very special shop! The architect, Szotynscy Zaleski, got the idea from a children's book. It is very unusual.

Writing

A. Look at this plan of a house. Complete the paragraph.

This is a plan of a house. There is a small kitchen. In the kitchen there is a _____, and a refrigerator. The kitchen is next to the _____ room. In the dining room there is a table with six chairs. The living room is _____ the dining room. There is a sofa and two armchairs in the living room. There are two _____ in the house—one big bedroom and a small bedroom. There is a _____ in the big bedroom.

B. Now write about your house.

In my house there is . . .

✓ **Goal 4** | **Compare houses**

Work with a partner. Take turns. Compare your own house with the houses in the reading.

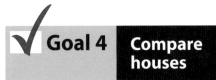

There is one bedroom in the tree house. There are three bedrooms in my house.

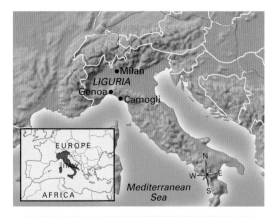

Before You Watch

A. Complete the video summary. Use the words in the box.

| fishermen   artists   village   paint   Sea   art |

Video summary

Camogli is a small town or _____ in Italy. Camogli is next to the Mediterranean _____. Many people in Camogli are _____. Their job is to catch fish. There are also _____ in Camogli. They _____ houses and buildings. Their _____ is called *trompe l'oeil*. It is very special. The paintings are very realistic. They make things look real, but they are not.

B. Look at the picture. Study the different parts of the house. Tell a partner which parts of the house are the same as your house or apartment.

There are three windows.

My house has . . .

C. Discuss the pictures with a partner. Which is real? Which is the *trompe l'oeil*?

While You Watch

 A. Watch the video. Match the parts of the sentences.

1. Artists use *trompe l'oeil* to make___   a. with bright colors.
2. People like to paint their houses ___   b. artists.
3. The fishermen painted their houses ___   c. things look real
4. Raffaella and Carlo are ___   d. from the sea.
5. You can see the houses of Camogli ___   e. with *trompe l'oeil* art.

 B. Watch the video again. Circle **T** for *true* and **F** for *false*.

1. Camogli is a large city.   T   F
2. In Camogli people paint their houses in bright colors.   T   F
3. The houses in Camogli are very special.   T   F
4. All the artists in Italy use *trompe l'oeil* technique.   T   F
5. Only fishermen paint their houses with *trompe l'oeil* art. T   F

▲ This wall is a *trompe l'oeil* painting.

After You Watch

Work with a partner. Take turns describing the changes you would make to your house with *trompe l'oeil*.

I want to add two balconies.

POSSESSIONS

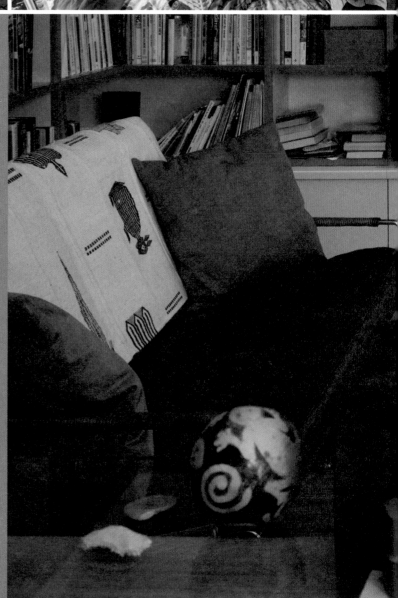

1. Do you have any of these things?

2. What is your favorite personal possession?

UNIT GOALS

Identify personal possessions
Talk about personal possessions
Buy a present
Talk about special possessions

Vocabulary

A. Complete the names of the objects in the pictures. Use the words in the box.

book	pen	watch	bag	glasses	handbag
wallet	ring	keys	necklace	dictionary	notebook

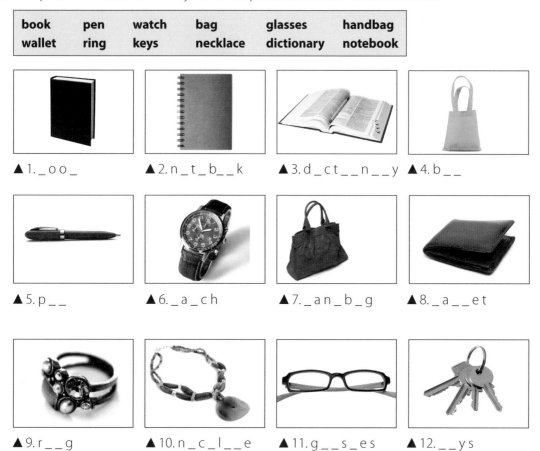

▲ 1. _ o o _

▲ 2. n _ t _ b _ _ k

▲ 3. d _ c t _ _ n _ _ y

▲ 4. b _ _

▲ 5. p _ _

▲ 6. _ a _ c h

▲ 7. _ a n _ b _ g

▲ 8. _ a _ _ e t

▲ 9. r _ _ g

▲ 10. n _ c _ l _ _ e

▲ 11. g _ _ s _ e s

▲ 12. _ _ y s

> There are glasses in my picture.

> There are no glasses in my picture, but there's a cell phone.

 B. Take turns. Find the differences between the two pictures.

STUDENT A

STUDENT B

Grammar: Demonstrative adjectives

	Singular	Plural	Possessive nouns
Near 👉	**This** is your bag.	Are **these** your books?	It's Jim**'s** bag.
Far 👉	**That** is not your bag.	**Those** are not my pens.	

A. Match the questions and the answers. There is more than one right answer.

Question
1. Is this your pen? _____
2. Are those your keys? _____
3. Are these your glasses? _____
4. Is that your dictionary? _____

Answer
a. Yes, they are.
b. No, it isn't. It's Peter's.
c. Yes, it is.
d. No, they aren't. They're Angie's.

B. Look at the pictures. Use the cues to write questions.

1. (far) _Are those your glasses?_
2. (far) _____
3. (near) _____
4. (near) _____
5. (far) _____

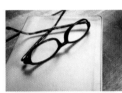
1.

2.

3.

4.

5.

Conversation

A. Listen to the conversation. What is in the bag?

Track 1-18

Andrea: Is this your bag?
Jennifer: No, *that's* my bag
Andrea: Maybe it's Jim's.
Jennifer: Let's look inside. There's a <u>book, a dictionary, a pen, a wallet</u> ...
Andrea: A <u>wallet</u>? Look inside.
Jennifer: Right, it's Jim's bag.

B. Practice the conversation with a partner. Switch roles and practice it again.

C. Change the underlined words and make a new conversation.

✓ Goal 1   Identify personal possessions

Describe the contents of your bag to a partner.

▲ Gill

▲ Lee

Listening

Track 1-19

A. Listen. Circle **T** for *true* and **F** for *false*.

1. There is cell phone in Gill's bag.   T   F
2. There is a dictionary in Gill's bag.   T   F
3. There is a cell phone in Lee's bag.   T   F
4. There is a notebook in Lee's bag.   T   F

Track 1-19

B. Listen again. Answer the questions.

1. What does Gill have in her bag that Lee doesn't have in his bag? _____
2. What does Gill have in her bag that Lee has in his bag? _____
3. What does Lee have in his bag that Gill doesn't have in her bag? _____

C. Work with a partner. Take turns. Ask and answer the questions.

1. What does Gill have in her bag that you don't have in your bag?
2. What does Gill have in her bag that you have in your bag?
3. What does Lee have in his bag that you don't have in your bag?
4. What does Lee have in his bag that you have in your bag?

Pronunciation: Short *i* and long *e* sound

A. Listen and check the boxes.

	long *e* sound	short *i* sound
this		
these		
heat		
hit		
his		
he's		
sheep		
ship		

▲ sheep

▲ ship

B. Listen again and repeat the words.

Communication

1. Write the name of an object on a small piece of paper. Give the paper to your teacher.
2. Your teacher mixes the papers and gives you someone else's paper
3. Find the owner.

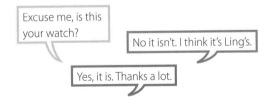

Excuse me, is this your watch?

No it isn't. I think it's Ling's.

Yes, it is. Thanks a lot.

Goal 2	**Talk about personal possessions**

Ask a partner about what is in his/her bag

Is there a pencil in your bag?

Language Expansion: Electronic products

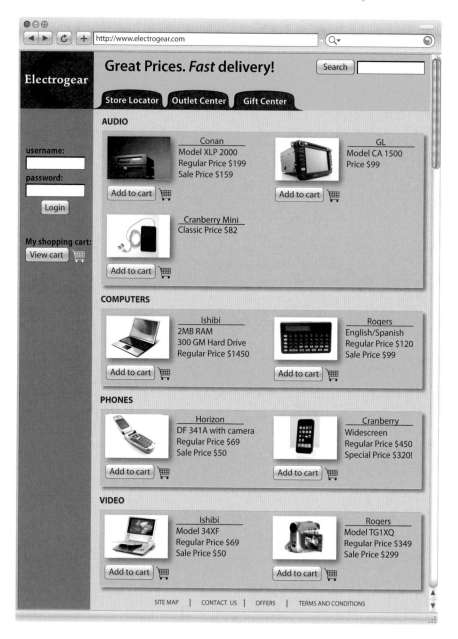

A. Label the items on the Web page. Use the words in the box.

CD player	**DVD player**	**cell phone**	**laptop**	**electronic dictionary**
camcorder	**touch phone**	**MP3 player**	**car audio**	

B. Read the Web page. Complete the sentences.

1. The camcorder is in the __Video__ section.
2. The _____ and the _____ are in the Phones section.
3. The electronic dictionary is in the _____ section.
4. The MP3 player is in the _____ section.

Grammar: *Have*

Statements	Negative
I/you/we/they **have** a laptop.	I/you/we/they **don't have** a CD player.
He/she **has** a camcorder.	He/she **doesn't have** a DVD player.
Yes/no questions	**Short answers**
Do I/you/we/they **have** an MP3 player?	Yes, I/you/we/they **do**. No, I/you/we/they **don't**.
Does he/she **have** a cell phone?	Yes, he/she **does**. No, he/she **doesn't**.

A. Complete the sentences with *have* or *has*.

1. Jim ___has___ a new laptop.
2. Do you _____ a touch phone?
3. I don't _____ a cell phone.
4. Does Chen _____ a DVD player?
5. Alan _____ a camcorder.

B. Write questions with *have*.

1. you/cell phone? _Do you have a cell phone?_____
2. Alison/big house? _____
3. you/my keys? _____
4. Aki/a laptop? _____
5. Mario and Linda/an apartment? _____

Conversation

Track 1-21

A. Sun-Hee and Hana are buying a present for Sun-Hee's brother. Listen to the conversation. What do they buy?

Sun-Hee:	Look at these new products!
Hana:	Wow, these <u>cameras</u> look cool. And cheap!
Sun-Hee:	My brother already has a good <u>camera</u>.
Hana:	Does he have <u>a touch phone</u>?
Sun-Hee:	No he doesn't. Let's get <u>a touch phone</u>!

 B. Practice the conversation with a partner. Switch roles and practice it again.

 C. Change the underlined words and make a new conversation.

Real Language

We use *Wow! Cool!* to show interest. Both are informal.

 **Goal 3** **Buy a present**

Work with a partner. Practice buying a present for a friend. Use the conversation and the Web site for ideas.

Reading

👥 **A.** These people are wearing traditional jewelry. Some people say they are beautiful. Other people say they are not beautiful and think they are ugly. Discuss your opinions with a partner.

📖 **B.** Read the sentences. Circle **T** for *true* and **F** for *false*.

1. Aisha's father is an
   important man.   T   F
2. Her jewelry is not made
   from gold.   T   F
3. The earrings are very old.   T   F
4. The necklaces come
   from Europe.   T   F
5. The bracelets are made
   of silver   T   F

C. Read and answer the questions.

1. Where does Aisha come from?

   _____

2. How old are the necklace and pendants?

   _____

3. Where do the earrings come from?

   _____

4. What is the Viking jewelry made of ?

   _____

☐ Jewelry

Jewelry is beautiful. In every country and in every age, people have jewelry.

Aisha comes from Djibouti. Her father is an important man. She has a lot of jewelry. It is made from gold.

These are earrings. They are from Kiev and are 1,500 years old. They are large and very beautiful.

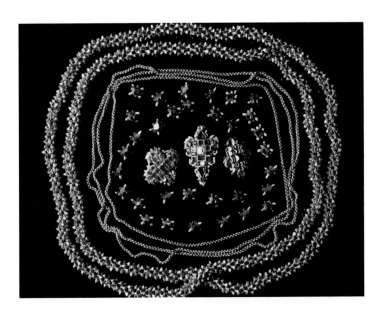

This is jewelry from the ship the *Concepción*. It is about 300 years old. There are two beautiful necklaces and three pendants. We think they come from Asia, but we are not sure.

This is Viking jewelry from Norway. It is made of silver. It is about 1,000 years old. There are chains and bracelets.

Communication

Work with a partner to complete the chart.

1. Fill in the first column with your information.
2. Fill in the second column with your partner's information.
3. Fill in the third column about your partner's best friend.

Do you have a CD player?

Yes, I do.

No, I don't.

Do you have . . .	Me	My partner	My partner's best friend
a CD player?			
a laptop computer?			
an electronic dictionary?			
a necklace?			
earrings?			
an MP3 player?			

Does he/she have earrings?

Yes, he/she does.

No, he/she doesn't.

Writing

Write about your partner. Use the information in the chart.

My partner has a CD player, a laptop computer, and a video camcorder. She doesn't have an electronic dictionary, a calculator, or an MP3 player.

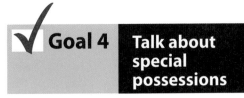

✓ **Goal 4** | **Talk about special possessions**

Work with a partner. Tell your partner about a special possession. What is it? Where is it from? Is it old or new?

Before You Watch

Work with a partner. Decide which of these things are interesting to archeologists.

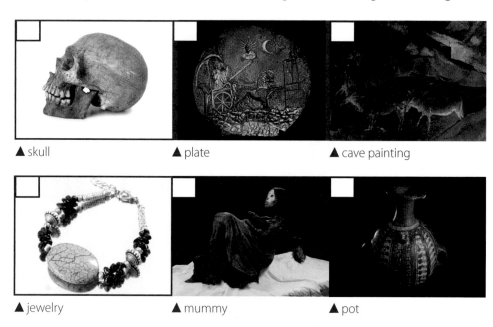

▲ skull

▲ plate

▲ cave painting

▲ jewelry

▲ mummy

▲ pot

While You Watch

 A. Watch the video. Check the pictures that you see on page 48.

 B. Watch again and complete the sentences from the video using the words in the box.

paintings   interesting   skulls   old   slow

1. They are looking for _____ things.
2. Archeologists also study human remains, like these _____.
3. It is _____ work.
4. Archeologists study _____ in caves.
5. Sometimes the work is dangerous, but it is always _____.

After You Watch

A. Match the tools to the job. There can be more than one right answer.

TOOLS

a. broom   b. ruler   c. brush   d. hammer

1. architect ____
2. artist ____
3. archeologist ____

 B. Compare your answers with a partner's answers.

DAILY ACTIVITIES

1. Which of these things do you do every day?

2. What other things do you do every day?

UNIT GOALS

Tell time
Talk about people's daily activities
Talk about what you do at work
Describe a job

Vocabulary

▲ get up

▲ take a shower

▲ start work

▲ finish work

▲ six o'clock

▲ six thirty, half past six

▲ take a nap

▲ go to bed

▲ have lunch

▲ have dinner

▲ six fifteen, a quarter after six

▲ five forty-five, a quarter to six

A. What time is it? Write the time.

1. It's five o'clock   2. _____   3. _____   4. _____   5. _____

B. Complete the sentences with your own information.

1. I get up at _____ .
2. I take a shower at _____ .
3. I start work at _____ .

4. I finish work at _____ .
5. I go to bed at _____ .

Grammar: Simple present tense—statements and negatives

Statement	Negative	What time . . . ?
I/you/we/they **get up** at seven o'clock. He/she **gets up** at seven thirty.	I/you/we/they **don't go** to work on Saturday. He/she **doesn't go** to bed at nine thirty.	What time **do** I/you/we/they **start** work? What time **does** he/she **start** work?
*The simple present tense is used for actions that we do every day.		

Time expressions with the simple present tense

every day/morning/afternoon/evening
at three o'clock
in the morning/the afternoon/the evening
on Sunday

A. Complete the sentences. Use the verbs in parentheses.

1. Alan _gets up_____ (get up) at eight o'clock.
2. I _____ (start) work at seven thirty in the evening.
3. We _____ (not take a nap) in the afternoon.
4. Wendy and Kate _____ (not have lunch) at one o'clock.
5. Dae-Ho _____ (finish) work at two o'clock every day.

B. Unscramble the sentences.

1. take a nap/I/in the afternoon _I take a nap in the afternoon_____ .
2. does not/at eight o'clock/Helen/start work _____ .
3. at one thirty/have lunch/We _____ .
4. morning/I/every/take a shower _____ .
5. work/finishes/at five o'clock/Paul _____ .

Conversation

Track 1-22

A. Listen to the conversation. What time does Mariana go to bed Sunday through Thursday?

Abel: What time do you get up?
Mariana: I get up at seven thirty Monday through Friday.
Abel: And on the weekend?
Mariana: I get up at about ten o'clock.
Abel: And what time do you go to bed?
Mariana: Sunday through Thursday, at about eleven o'clock, but on the weekend . . . late!

 B. Practice the conversation with a partner. Switch roles and practice it again.

C. Practice the conversation again. Use your own information.

> What time does your mother get up?

> She gets up at six thirty.

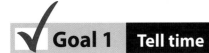
✓ Goal 1   Tell time

Work with a partner. Ask and answer time questions about a friend or relative.

▲ Joel Sartore at work

▲ photograph by Joel Sartore

▲ photograph by Joel Sartore

Listening

Track 1-23

A. Look at the photos. What is Joel's job? Listen to the interview and check your answer.

Track 1-23

B. Listen again and answer the questions.

1. What is Joel's job? _____

2. What time does he get up? _____

3. What time does he take a nap? _____

4. What time does he take photos? _____

Sunday

Monday
6:30 take bird photos
at beach

Tuesday
7:30 p.m. sunset photos
at beach

Wednesday

Thursday
9:15 meet Jane F. — interview

Friday
lunch with Michael

Saturday

Word Focus

take a photo =
use a camera

What do you
do on Monday?

I go to class at
8 o'clock.

C. Work with a partner. Take turns asking and answering questions about what you do every day.

Pronunciation: Falling intonation on statements and information questions

A. Listen and repeat.

Track 1-24

1. What time do you get up? ↘ I get up at six o'clock. ↘

2. What time do they have lunch? ↘ They have lunch at one thirty. ↘

3. What time does Bill go to bed? ↘ He goes to bed at eleven o'clock. ↘

 B. Take turns reading the following questions and answers to a partner.

1. What time does Salma start work? She starts work at eight thirty.
2. What time do they get up? They get up at a quarter to seven.
3. What time do you finish work? I finish work at six o'clock.

Communication

1. Write two more questions.
2. Answer all the questions.
3. Ask two classmates the questions.

Alison gets up at eight o'clock.

She has breakfast at nine thirty.

What time do you . . .	Me	Classmate 1	Classmate 2
1. get up?			
2. have breakfast?			
3. start work?			
4. _____			
5. _____			

 Goal 2 **Talk about people's daily activities**

Tell a partner about your classmates' activities.

Language Expansion: Work Activities

 ▲ check emails

 ▲ meet clients

 ▲ go to meetings

 ▲ travel

 ▲ talk to people on the phone

 ▲ make photocopies

 ▲ go to the bank

 ▲ fill out forms

A. Write the activities in the correct column.

Things I do every day.	Things I do every week.	Things I don't do.
I check my emails.		

B. What other things do you do at work? Make a list. Then tell a partner.

Grammar: Simple present tense—questions and answers

Question	Short answer
Do I/you/we/they **meet** clients every day?	Yes, I/you/we/they **do**. No, I/you/we/they **don't**.
Does he/she **meet** clients every day?	Yes, he/she **does**. No, he/she **doesn't**.

Adverbs of frequency

I **always** check my emails.	100%
I **sometimes** meet clients.	50%
I **never** answer the phone.	0%

A. Match the questions and the answers.

Questions

1. Do you meet clients every day? ___
2. Does Alan meet clients every day? ___
3. Do Chris and Helen travel a lot? ___
4. Does Hilary go to the bank every day? ___
5. Do you go to meetings every day? ___

Answers

a. Yes, they do.
b. No she doesn't. She goes every week.
c. No, I don't. I never meet clients.
d. Yes, I do.
e. Yes, he does.

B. Write about your work. Complete the sentences using *always*, *sometimes*, *never*.

1. I _____ check my emails at nine o'clock.
2. I _____ go to meetings on Mondays.
3. I _____ make photocopies.
4. I _____ go to the bank.
5. I _____ fill out forms.

Conversation

Track 1-25

A. Listen to the conversation. What does Brenda do at work?

Yoshi: Tell me about your work.
Brenda: Well, I'm a <u>personal assistant at a travel agency</u>.
Yoshi: What do you do at work?
Brenda: Oh, I <u>check my boss's emails. I make photocopies. I go to the bank</u>. It's not very interesting.
Yoshi: Do you travel?
Brenda: Sometimes. <u>I go to meetings with my boss, like to Rio and Singapore</u>.
Yoshi: Not interesting! It sounds fantastic to me.

 B. Practice the conversation with a partner. Switch roles and practice it again.

 C. Change the underlined words and make a new conversation.

Goal 3   **Talk about what you do at work**

Talk to a partner about what you do at work.

Word Focus

boss = your superior, the person at the top

Real Language

We can use *like* to give examples.

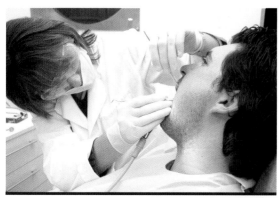

▲ dentist

astronaut ▶

Reading

A. Work with a partner to answer these questions.

What do these people do at work? What are their working hours? Can a robot do their work?

B. Read. Circle **T** for *true* or **F** for *false*.

1. Robots have long holidays.　　T　F
2. Robots finish work at five o'clock.　　T　F
3. Working under the sea is a problem for robots.　　T　F
4. The police use robots.　　T　F
5. There are robots in outer space.　T　F

Robots at Work

> **Job Description**
> **Working Hours:** 24 hours a day, every day
> **Salary:** $0
> **Holidays:** None
> **Duties:** Welding cars

What a job! It's not a job description for a person. It's a job description for a robot. Robots don't eat, they don't take naps, and they don't go to bed. They work 24 hours a day— every day. They are very useful.

▲ A robot welds a car in a Japanese car factory.

This robot works under the sea. It is dangerous for people but it is not a problem for a robot.

A policeman's work is sometimes dangerous. This is a bomb squad. They use robots to look for bombs.

It is expensive and dangerous to send a man to outer space, but it is easy work for this robot.

Writing

Read this job description, and then write a job description for yourself or for a friend.

Job Description: Personal Assistant
Working Hours: 9:00 a.m. to 5:00 p.m., Monday to Friday
Holidays: Public holidays + 10 vacation days per year
Duties: Answer the phone. Make photocopies. Write emails. Meet clients.

Communication

Ask your classmates about the job description they wrote.

What hours do you (or does your friend) work?

What holidays do you (or does your friend) have?

What do you (or does your friend) do at work?

Goal 4　**Describe a job**

Tell a partner about a job you want to do.

Before You Watch

A. Look at the pictures. Which of these jobs is difficult? Which of these jobs is routine?

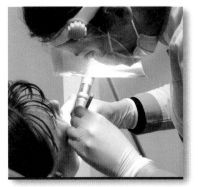

▲ A dentist treats a patient in her office.

▲ Dentists treat a tiger at the zoo.

B. Read the Video Summary. Use the words in blue to label the pictures.

Video Summary

Two dentists go to the San Francisco Zoo to treat animals. Their first patient is a **sea lion** named Artie. Artie eats 20 pounds of fish a day. His **teeth** are fine. Then they examine an **elephant** named Sue. They check teeth and **molars** in her **mouth** and her tusks. Their last patient is a very difficult patient. She is a **black jaguar** with a **toothache**. Sandy's teeth are very bad and she needs surgery. The dentists have a very hard day.

Word Focus

routine = something you do every day

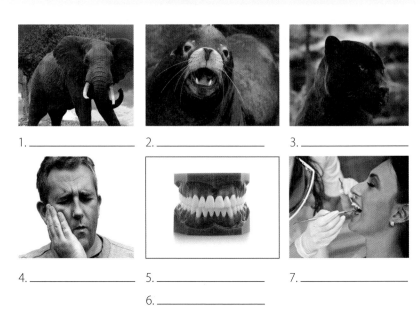

1. _____   2. _____   3. _____

4. _____   5. _____   7. _____

6. _____

While You Watch

A. Watch the video. Check the activities that you see.
- ☐ take an X-ray
- ☐ examine a patient
- ☐ clean teeth
- ☐ check gums
- ☐ anesthetize a patient
- ☐ perform surgery

Word Focus

anesthetize = make a patient sleep
check up = a medical or dental examination
filling = covering for a hole in a tooth

B. Watch again. Complete the sentences. Use *always*, *sometimes*, or *never*.

1. Dr. Sarah de Sanz _____ treats human patients.
2. Dr. Brown's animal patients are _____ dangerous.
3. Animals_____ have dental problems.
4. Most dentists_____ treat animals.
5. Humans and animals _____ need good teeth.

After You Watch

Ask two classmates these questions about their personal routines.

	Classmate 1	Classmate 2
1. Do you get up at the same time every day?		
2. Do you have the same breakfast every day?		
3. Do you go to work at the same time every day?		
4. Do you do the same things at work every day?		
5. Do you go to bed at the same time every day?		

GETTING THERE

1. How do you travel to work?

2. What other types of transportation do you use?

UNIT GOALS

Ask for and give directions
Create and use a tour route
Talk about transportation
Record a journey

Vocabulary

A. Work with a partner. Locate these places on the map.

> There is a tourist office on Grand Street.

tourist office	**train station**	**supermarket**	**post office**	**library**
restaurant	**hotel**	**park**	**museum**	**bank**
art gallery	**bus station**	**movie theater**	**shopping mall**	

B. Read the directions and follow the red arrow.

Directions

You are in the tourist office. Cross Lincoln Avenue. Walk two blocks and cross Long Avenue. Turn left and walk two blocks. Turn right and go into the museum.

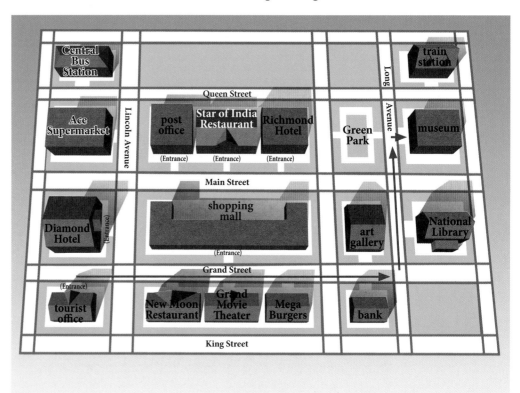

C. Follow the directions and write the destination.

1. From the tourist office walk two blocks up Lincoln Avenue. Turn right on Main Street. Walk two blocks and turn left into _Green Park_ .

2. From Central Bus Station walk one block down Lincoln Avenue, turn left on Main Street, walk two blocks, cross Long Avenue, and you are at the _____ _____ .

3. From the Diamond Hotel, cross Lincoln Avenue, walk two blocks to the art gallery. Cross Grand Street and you are at the _____ .

Grammar: Imperatives

Positive	Negative
Turn right.	**Don't turn** left.

*The imperative is used for giving instructions.

Prepositions of place
on the corner of
across from
between

► The Diamond Hotel is **on the corner of** Lincoln Avenue and Grand Street.

A. Write the positive or negative imperative.

1. At the end of the block, ___don't turn___ (turn) right, turn left.
2. _____ (walk) for three blocks and then turn right.
3. _____ (go) to the bank, go to the post office.
4. _____ (cross) the street and turn left.
5. _____ (take a nap). It's time for lunch.

► The art gallery is **across from** the library.

B. Use the map, and write the correct prepositions.

1. The art gallery is _____ Long Avenue and Main Street.
2. The museum is _____ Green Park.
3. The Grand Movie Theater is _____ Mega Burgers and the New Moon Restaurant.
4. The tourist office is _____ Grand Street and Lincoln Avenue.
5. The post office is _____ the Ace Supermarket.

► There is a restaurant **between** the post office and the Richmond Hotel.

Conversation

Track 1-26

A. A guest at the Richmond Hotel is talking to the receptionist. Listen to the conversation. Where does the guest want to go?

Hotel Guest:	Is there a <u>supermarket</u> near here?
Receptionist:	There's one <u>on the corner of Lincoln Avenue and Main Street across from the post office</u>.
Hotel Guest:	How do I get there?
Receptionist:	OK. <u>Leave the hotel and turn right. Walk one block and cross Lincoln Avenue</u>.
Hotel Guest:	Thank you very much.
Receptionist:	You're welcome.

B. Practice the conversation with a partner. Switch roles and practice it again.

C. Change the underlined words and make a new conversation.

Real Language

To ask for directions, we say, *How do I get there?*

✓ Goal 1   Ask for and give directions

Work with a partner. Take turns asking for and giving directions using the map on page 64.

Listening

New York Window Displays

New York is expensive, but you can look at the store windows for free. Take a walking tour around New York's top stores.

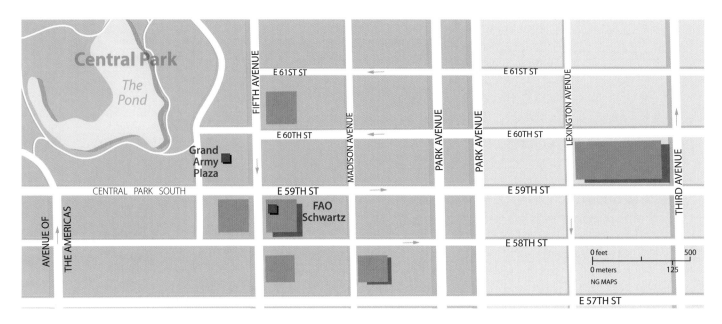

A. Write the names of the stores on the map.

1. **Bergdorf Goodman** is on East 58th Street, across from the Grand Army Plaza.
2. **FAO Schwartz** is on the corner of East 58th Street and 5th Avenue.
3. **Barneys New York** is on the corner of East 61st Street and 5th Avenue.
4. **Tiffany & Co.** is on East 57th Street and 5th Avenue.
5. **Bloomingdale's** is on the corner of East 60th Street and Lexington Avenue.

B. Listen. Draw the route on the map.

Track 1-27

Pronunciation: of *yes/no* questions

A. Listen and repeat.

Track 1-28

1. Is there a movie theater near here? Yes, there is.

2. Is the bus station on York Street? No, it isn't.

3. Is Barneys on the corner of East 61st Street and 5th Avenue? Yes, it is.

B. Take turns reading the questions and answers.

A: Is there a hotel near here?
B: No, there isn't.
A: Is the library next to the museum?
B: Yes, it is.
A: Is there a tourist office in this town?
B: No, there isn't.

Communication

Use the map on page 66. Ask for and give these directions to a partner.

1. From Barneys New York to Tiffany & Co.
2. From Bergdorf Goodman to Barneys New York.
3. From Bergdorf Goodman to Bloomingdale's.
4. From Tiffany & Co. to Bloomingdale's.

✓ **Goal 2** **Create and use a tour route**

Work together and write a tour route in your town.

Language Expansion: Ground Transportation

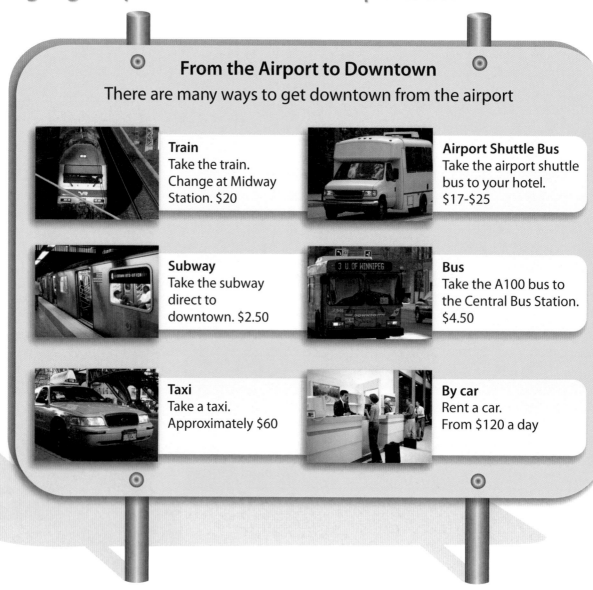

From the Airport to Downtown

There are many ways to get downtown from the airport

Train
Take the train. Change at Midway Station. $20

Airport Shuttle Bus
Take the airport shuttle bus to your hotel. $17-$25

Subway
Take the subway direct to downtown. $2.50

Bus
Take the A100 bus to the Central Bus Station. $4.50

Taxi
Take a taxi. Approximately $60

By car
Rent a car. From $120 a day

A. Complete the chart with the names of different ground transportation.

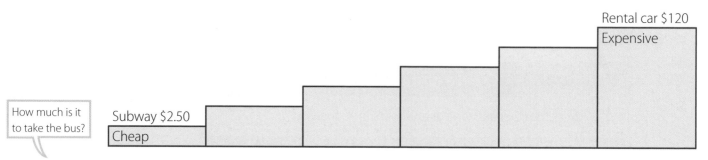

Rental car $120
Expensive

How much is it to take the bus?

Subway $2.50
Cheap

B. Work with a partner. Ask and answers questions about how much it costs to travel from the airport.

Grammar: *Have to*

Statement	Question	Short answer
I/you/we/they **have to** take a taxi.	**Do** I/you/we/they **have to** change trains?	Yes, I/you/we/they **do.** No, I/you/we/they **don't.**
He/she **has to** change buses.	**Does** he/she **have to** take a taxi?	Yes, he/she **does.** No, he/she **doesn't.**

*****Have to** is used to show obligation.

A. Complete the sentences with the correct form of *have to*.

1. You <u>*have to*</u> take a bus.
2. We _____ take the subway.
3. She _____ take a taxi.
4. They _____ go to the bank
5. Susan _____ check her emails.

B. Write questions using *have to*.

1. <u>*Do we have to*</u> (we) change trains
2. _____ (I) take a train?
3. _____ (they) go to the meeting?
4. _____ (you) change trains?
5. _____ (Bill) cross the street?

Conversation

Track 1-29

A. Listen to the conversation. What time does the plane leave?

Tourist: Excuse me, how do I get to the airport?

Assistant: You can take <u>the subway</u>, but you have to change <u>trains</u>. It takes about an hour.

Tourist: Oh! But I have to get there by two thirty. And I have four bags!

Assistant: Two thirty! In half an hour? OK, you have to take <u>a taxi</u>! And quickly!

B. Practice the conversation with a partner. Switch roles and practice it again.

C. Change the underlined words and make a new conversation.

✓ **Goal 3**   **Talk about transportation**

Take turns giving directions from one place to another in your town. Say what transportation you have to take.

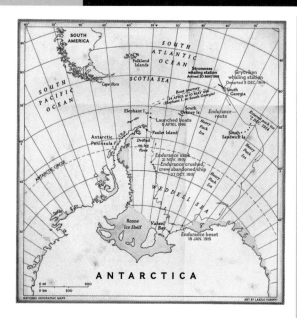

Reading

 A. Read the diary and follow the route on the map.

B. Choose the correct answer.

1. The journey starts in __.
   a. Elephant Island
   b. London
   c. South Georgia
2. The *Endurance* breaks up on ___.
   a. October 26, 1914
   b. October 26, 1915
   c. October 26, 1916
3. __ men leave Elephant Island on a small boat.
   a. Four
   b. Five
   c. Six
4. It takes __ to sail from Elephant Island to South Georgia.
   a. one week
   b. two weeks
   c. three weeks
5. Shackleton finds help in ___.
   a. Stromness
   b. Elephant Island
   c. London

Antarctica

Shackleton's Epic Journey—A diary

1914

August 8 Ernest Shackleton and his men leave London on their ship, *Endurance*.

1915

January 18 The *Endurance* is trapped in the ice. The men play soccer.
October 26 The *Endurance* **breaks up**. The men have to leave the *Endurance*. They camp on the ice.

1916

April 9 The ice begins to break up. They have to get into the small boats.

April 15 They land on Elephant Island.

April 24 Shackleton and five men leave Elephant Island in a small boat to find **help**. The other men stay on Elephant Island.

May 8 Shackleton lands in South Georgia.

May 19 Shackleton leaves three men with the boat. He crosses the mountains of South Georgia with two other men to find help.

May 20 They arrive in Stromness, the main town in South Georgia. They find help.

August 30 Shackleton **rescues** the men on Elephant Island.

Word Focus

rescue = save
break up = to fall to pieces
help = assistance

Writing

Write a diary about a real or imaginary journey.

> June 3: We leave the airport at one o'clock. We change planes. We arrive at the hotel at eleven o'clock.
> June 4: We take the subway to the museum. In the afternoon, we walk to the art gallery.

_____

_____

_____

_____

_____

_____

_____

_____

_____

_____

_____

_____

_____

✓ **Goal 4** | **Record a journey**

Share your diary entry with the class.

Before You Watch

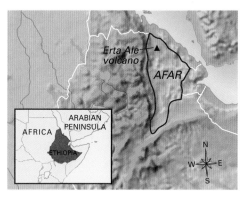

A. Study the picture. Use the words to complete the text.

> A volcano is a mountain with a large hole at the top. This hole is called a _____. A volcano produces very hot, melted rock. When it is under ground, this hot, melted rock is called _____. When it leaves or comes out of the volcano, it is called _____. When the lava stays in the crater it forms a _____.
>
> When lava leaves a volcano, we say the volcano erupts. We call it an _____.

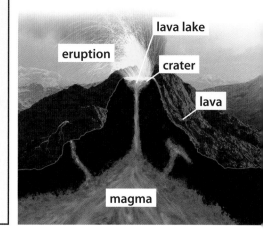

B. Work with a partner. Read the definitions and label the pictures.

explorers = people who go to new places to learn things

geologists = scientists who study the earth (rocks and soil)

trek = a long and difficult trip or journey

camel = a large animal that can travel through the desert

professor = a teacher at a university.

▲ rocks and soil

_____   _____   _____   _____   _____

While You Watch

A. Watch the video. Match the sentence parts.

1. The geologists _____
2. The lava lake _____
3. Hot lava comes out of the earth _____
4. The team spends hours _____
5. It is not easy to stand near the crater _____
6. The professors are _____

a. collecting pieces of red-hot lava.
b. travel to the volcano on camels.
c. excited about studying the volcano.
d. because it is very hot.
e. is inside the crater.
f. and forms the lava lake.

B. Watch the video again and answer these questions.

1. What can geologists study at Erta Ale? _____
2. Where does the red hot lava come from? _____
3. In the early morning, what is the temperature near the crater? _____
4. How does the team feel when they return from the volcano? _____

C. What did you learn? Discuss with a partner what you see in these photos?

After You Watch

Discuss these questions with a partner.

1. Do you want to explore a volcano?
2. Why or why not?
3. How can people travel to difficult places?

FREE TIME

1. What are these people doing?

2. What activities do you do in your free time?

UNIT GOALS

Identify activities that are happening now
Talk about activities that are happening now
Talk about abilities
Talk about sports

Vocabulary

Track 2-2

A. Listen and write the words from the box under the correct picture.

going to the movies drawing	watching TV going for a walk	playing the guitar listening to music	reading cooking

Katie	Lok	Ben	Omar

1. _watching TV_   2. _____   3. _____   4. _____

Mariko	Crystal	Tom and Susan	Tony

5. _____   6. _____   7. _____   8. _____

B. Write the activities in exercise **A** in the correct column.

I like	I don't like

Grammar: Present continuous tense

Statement (negative)	*Yes/no* question	Short answer	*Wh-* question
I **am (not) reading**.	**Am** I **reading**?	Yes, I am. No, I'm not.	Where am I going?
You/we/they **are (not) reading**.	**Are** you/we/they **reading**?	Yes, you/we/they are. No, you/we/they aren't.	What are you/we/they doing?
He/she **is (not) reading**.	**Is** he/she **reading**?	Yes, he/she is. No, he/she isn't.	What is he/she doing?

*We use the present continuous tense to talk about things that are happening at the moment.

A. Unscramble the words to write sentences.

1. the guitar / is playing / Charlie _____
2. Marian / watching TV / is not _____
3. is listening / Asha / to music _____
4. cooking lunch / is not / Bernardo _____
5. Ju / drawing / Is _____

B. Complete the conversation.

Dan: Is Miriam _____ TV?
Beth: No, she _____ .
Dan: What is she _____ ?
Beth: _____ drawing.

 C. Take turns practicing the conversation in exercise **B** with a partner. Use the pictures on page 76.

Conversation

 A. Listen to the phone call. What is Dave doing?

Track 2-3

Dave: Hi, Mom.
Mom: Dave! Where are you? What are you doing?
Dave: Mom, don't worry! I'm at <u>Paul's</u>. We're <u>listening to music</u>.
Mom: Well, don't be home late.
Dave: Mom, I'm <u>17</u> years old. Chill!

 B. Practice the conversation with a partner. Switch roles and practice it again.

C. Change the underlined words and make a new conversation.

Real Language

We can use these expressions to tell someone not to worry.

Formal ←————————→ Informal
Don't worry!   Relax!   Take it easy!   Chill!

 Goal 1 **Identify activities that are happening now**

What is he/she doing?

Work with a partner. Look at the pictures on page 76. Ask and answer questions.

Listening

A. Look at the pictures and listen to the telephone conversations. In what order do you hear the conversations? Write the number.

Track 2-4

B. Answer the questions. Listen again to check your answers.

Track 2-4

1. What is Mike doing? _____
2. Is Dave's wife taking a walk? _____
3. What is she doing? _____
4. Is Salma playing the guitar? _____
5. What is she doing? _____

Pronunciation: *sh* and *ch* sounds

Track 2-5

A. Listen and check the word you hear.

1. watch ✓   wash
2. cheap   sheep
3. chair   share
4. chip   ship
5. cash   catch
6. chop   shop
7. choose   shoes

B. Take turns reading the words. Your partner points to the words you say.

Communication

Work with a partner. Imagine that you are talking on the phone to each other. Have a conversation about what you are doing right now. Be creative.

 Goal 2   **Talk about activities that are happening now**

Work with a partner. Take turns talking about what a friend or family member is doing right now.

Language Expansion: Sports

A. Match the words in the box to the pictures.

ice skate	ski	play soccer	play tennis
play volleyball	play golf	swim	play football

1. _____ 2. _____ 3. _____ 4. _____

5. _____ 6. _____ 7. _____ 8. _____

B. Answers the questions. Then interview two classmates.

Do you . . .	Me	Classmate 1	Classmate 2
play soccer?			
ski?			
ice skate?			
play golf?			
play tennis?			
swim?			
play volleyball?			
play football?			

Grammar: *Can* for ability

Statement	Negative	*Yes/no* question	Short answer
I/you/she/we/they **can** swim.	He **can't** play the guitar.	**Can** you ski?	Yes, I **can**. No, I **can't**.

A. Write about yourself. Complete the sentences with *can* or *can't*.

1. I _____ swim.
2. I _____ play soccer.
3. I _____ play golf.
4. I _____ ski.
5. I _____ play tennis.

B. Complete the conversations.

1. **A:** _____ play volleyball?
   B: No, I can't but I _____ play football.
2. **A:** _____ Damien swim?
   B: Yes, _____.

Conversation

Track 2-6

A. Listen to the conversation. What can Yumi's boyfriend do?

Julie: Hi, Yumi. I hear you have a new boyfriend.
Yumi: Yes, he's cute. He can <u>play the guitar</u>.
Julie: Wow!
Yumi: Yes, and he can <u>ski</u> and <u>ice skate</u>.
Julie: Hey! I can ski and ice skate.
Yumi: Sorry, Julie. He's taken!

 B. Practice the conversation with a partner. Switch roles and practice it again.

C. Change the underlined words and make a new conversation.

 Goal 3 **Talk about abilities**

Ask a partner questions. Find out what he or she can do.

Can you ski?

No, I can't but I can ice skate.

Sports— Then and Now

▲ gymnastics

▲ ski jumping

Percy Hodges, a British athlete, is jumping a hurdle in this photo. He is also carrying a tray of drinks.

Modern athletes can run very quickly, but they don't carry trays of drinks.

Reading

A. Look at the pictures. Which of these sports can you do?

 B. Read the article. Circle **T** for *true* and **F** for *false*.

1. Percy Hedge is a modern athlete.   T   F
2. Modern athletes don't carry
   trays of drinks.   T   F
3. Javier Sotomayor is a gymnast.   T   F
4. The high jump world record
   was 245 centimeters in 1912.   T   F
5. Many gymnasts are young.   T   F

In this photo from July 1936, Olympic champion Jesse Owens is jumping hurdles on board the ship *Manhattan*. He is traveling to the Olympic Games in Berlin.

The world record for the high jump in 1912 was 1 meter, 98 centimeters. Today Javier Sotomayor from Cuba is the world record holder. He can jump 2 meters, 45 centimeters.

This young Chinese boy is performing at a railway station in 1920.

Today many of the world's top gymnasts are very young, but it is not an easy life.

Writing

Write sentences about the things you can do and the things you can't do.

I can play basketball, but I can't swim.

_____

_____

_____

_____

_____

_____

_____

_____

_____

Communication

Look at the pictures on these pages. Take turns asking and answering questions about the activities.

What's she/he doing?

Can you do this?

✓ **Goal 4** **Talk about sports**

Work with a partner. Talk about your favorite sports. Say what sports you like to watch. Say what sports you like to play.

Before You Watch

People play sports and games . . .

▲ for money

▲ for exercise

▲ for fun

A. Why do people play these sports? Write the name of the sport in the correct column. You can write the name in more than one column.

▲ skateboarding   ▲ golf   ▲ jogging   ▲ bungee jumping   ▲ ski jumping

For money	For exercise	For fun

B. Why do you think the people of Vanuatu dive from a tower?

While You Watch

 A. Watch the video and check your answer to exercise **B** on page 84.

 B. Watch the video again. Circle **T** for *true* and **F** for *false*.

1. Bungee jumping started in New Zealand.　　　　T　　F
2. The tower is 40 feet high.　　　　　　　　　　T　　F
3. The men dive from the tower for money.　　　　T　　F
4. Land diving is not dangerous.　　　　　　　　T　　F
5. Only people from Vanuatu can jump from the tower.　T　　F

After You Watch

 Look at the pictures on page 84. Take turns asking each other these questions.

What is he/she doing?

Can you do this?

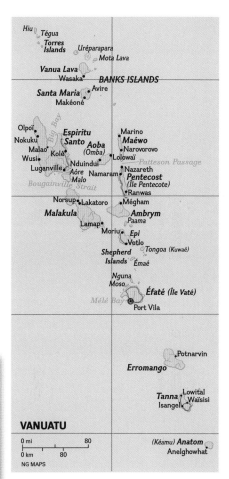

CLOTHES

1. Which of these clothes do you wear?

2. What colors can you see?

UNIT GOALS

Identify and buy clothes
Say what people are wearing
Express likes and dislikes
Learn about clothes and colors

Vocabulary

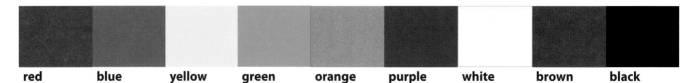

| red | blue | yellow | green | orange | purple | white | brown | black |

> This is a black hat.

A. Look at the color chart. Take turns describing the photos to a partner.

▲ shirt

▲ pants

▲ dress

▲ skirt

▲ shoes

▲ sweater

▲ jacket

▲ coat

▲ tie

▲ hat

B. Complete the sentences. Notice the words in **blue**.

1. Ruben is **trying on** a pair of _____.
2. Lucy is **paying** for the _____ **by** credit card.
3. The sales assistant is **bringing** more _____.

Grammar: *Can/could* (polite requests)

Can/could
Can I try it on, please?
Could you bring another pair, please?
*Can and could are used to make polite requests.

Write the polite requests.

1. You want to try on a blue dress. _Can I try on this blue dress, please?_
2. You want to see some red shoes. _____
3. You want to pay by credit card. _____
4. You want to try on a green sweater _____
5. You want the sales assistant to bring a size 7. _____

Conversation

Track 2-7

A. Listen to the conversation. What color shoes does the customer want?

Customer:	Do you have any white shoes?
Sales Assistant:	Yes, we do.
Customer:	Could I see them, please?
Sales Assistant:	Yes, of course.
Customer:	Ah, these look nice. Can I try them on, please?
Sales Assistant:	Sure.

B. Practice the conversation with a partner. Switch roles and practice it again.

Real Language

We can show we agree by saying:

Formal ◄————————————► Informal

Of course   Yes   Sure

 **Goal 1**   **Identify and buy clothes**

Work with a partner. Take turns role-playing a sales assistant and a customer. Buy some clothes.

Listening

Track 2-8

A. Listen to the descriptions. Match the names to the pictures.

| Helen | Dave | Zahra | Jenny |

Jenny is wearing . . .

1. _____

2. _____

3. _____

4. _____

B. Take turns describing the picture to a partner.

Pronunciation: *Could you*

Track 2-9

A. Listen and check (✓) the box of the form you hear.

	Full form	Short form
1. Could you call a taxi, please?	✓	
2. Could you call a taxi, please?		✓
3. Could you help me, please?		
4. Could you help me, please?		
5. Could you repeat that, please?		
6. Could you repeat that, please?		

 B. Take turns reading the following sentences using the short form.

1. Could you open the window, please?
2. Could you pass the water, please?
3. Could you say that again, please?
4. Could you tell me the time, please?
5. Could you open the door, please?
6. Could you repeat that, please?

Communication

 Take turns describing another classmate's clothing and guess the name of the classmate.

She is wearing blue pants and a red sweater.

It's Andrea.

That's right.

 Goal 2 **Say what people are wearing**

Find photos you like in this book. Tell a partner what people in the photos are wearing.

Language Expansion: More clothes and colors

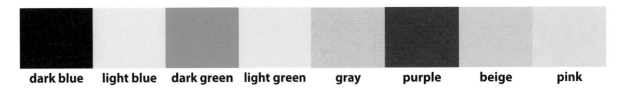

| dark blue | light blue | dark green | light green | gray | purple | beige | pink |

A. Write the colors of these clothes.

1. _light blue_ jeans 2. _____ socks 3. _____ blouse 4. _____ scarf 5. _____ t-shirt

B. Write all the clothes you know in the correct column.

Clothes men wear	Clothes women wear	Clothes men and women wear
		jeans

Grammar: Likes and dislikes

Likes and dislikes	
☺☺	I **love** jeans.
☺	I **like** pink t-shirts.
☹	I **don't like** hats.
☹☹	I **hate** white socks.

*We use these expressions to express likes and dislikes.

A. Complete the first column of the chart with other things that are not clothes. Then check (✓) the columns to show your likes and dislikes.

	☺☺ I love . . .	☺ I like . . .	☹ I don't like . . .	☹☹ I hate . . .
1. black jeans				
2. purple socks				
3. red clothes				
4.				
5.				
6.				
7.				
8.				

 B. Take turns asking about a partner's chart.

Conversation

Track 2-10

A. Chung and Brenda are buying a present for Brenda's boyfriend. Listen to the conversation. What present do they buy?

Chung: What clothes does he like?
Brenda: He likes casual clothes. Jeans and t-shirts, you know.
Chung: What colors does he like?
Brenda: He loves dark colors. He hates colors like yellow or white.
Chung: OK, so buy him a black t-shirt.

 B. Practice the conversation with a partner. Switch roles and practice it again.

 C. Practice the conversation again, but buy a present for a person that you both know.

What things do you love?
I love traveling.

✓ **Goal 3** **Express likes and dislikes**

Tell a partner about things you love and things you hate.

Reading

A. Tell a partner your favorite clothes color.

B. Match the word and the definition.

1. chameleon __
2. invisible __
3. to change __
4. soldier __
5. skin __

a. a person who fights in a war
b. an animal that changes color
c. the part of the body you can see
d. something you can't see
e. to make something different

C. Circle **T** for *true* and **F** for *false*.

1. Chameleons change color when they are angry.   T   F
2. Blue is a powerful color.   T   F
3. Pink is the color of love.   T   F
4. You can buy clothes that change color.   T   F
5. Soldiers are invisible.   T   F

Word Focus

powerful = strong
romantic = loving
calm = quiet

Chameleon Clothes

Chameleons can change the color of their skin. Sometimes they change color so they are difficult to see and become almost invisible. Sometimes they change color to show that they are angry or happy or looking for a partner.

Of course, humans can't change the color of their skin but we can change our clothes. Dark clothes make a person look more **powerful**. Pink is **romantic**; blue is **calm**. The color of your clothes says a lot about you.

Scientists are working on clothes that can change color when you press a button. They are not ready yet, but the idea is to make pants that can change from white to black or a shirt that can change from white to pink or red. Chameleon clothes!

But clothes that change color are also useful for soldiers. Like the chameleon, soldiers sometimes need to be invisible. Chameleon clothes make the soldiers difficult to see.

So, one day maybe you will be able to change your clothes from powerful to romantic to invisible, at the press of a button.

Writing

Write about what you or a classmate is wearing.

Ibrahim is wearing a brown shirt with a green sweater. He is also wearing black trousers and black shoes. I like his clothes. He looks great.

Communication

Take turns asking a partner about the clothes in the picture.

What is she wearing?

What color is it?

Do you like it?

Goal 4 **Learn about clothes and colors**

Ask your partner these questions.
What is your favorite color?
What are your favorite clothes?

Nunavut, CANADA

Before You Watch

We wear clothes . . .

▲ to be warm.

▲ to be dry.

▲ to carry things.

▲ to look good.

A. Why are these people wearing these clothes?

▲ fur coat

▲ fur pants

▲ vest

▲ evening gown

▲ waterproof gear

1. *She is wearing a fur coat to be warm and to look good*

2. _____

3. _____

4. _____

5. _____

While You Watch

 Watch the video. Circle the correct answers. There is more than one correct answer.

1. The models are wearing ___.
   a. hats
   b. jackets
   c. skirts
2. Aaju Peter is a ___.
   a. designer
   b. model
   c. photographer

3. Inuit women wear the Amouti to ___.
   a. be warm
   b. look good
   c. carry babies
4. Inuit kill seals for their ___.
   a. meat
   b. fur
   c. fat

After You Watch

The Inuit make clothes from seal fur. We also make clothes from other animals.

A. Match the animals and the material.

1. sheep _____   2. cow _____   3. rabbit _____

▲ fur   ▲ wool   ▲ leather

We make shoes from leather.

 B. Discuss with a partner what clothes we make from wool, leather, and fur.

EAT WELL

1. What food do you see in the pictures?

2. What is your favorite food?

UNIT GOALS

Order a meal
Plan a party
Talk about a healthy diet
Talk about food for special occasions

Vocabulary

▲ cereal   ▲ eggs   ▲ steak   ▲ fish

▲ salad   ▲ pasta   ▲ chicken   ▲ fruit juice

▲ coffee   ▲ tea   ▲ chocolate cake   ▲ ice cream

A. Write the food in the correct place on the menu.

Breakfast
(7:00 a.m. to 12:00 p.m.)

_____

_____

Lunch & Dinner
(12:00 p.m. to 8:00 p.m.)
All served with salad

_____

_____

Drinks

_____

_____

Desserts

_____

_____

B. Tell a partner what you like to eat for breakfast, lunch, and dinner.

Grammar: *Some* and *any*

Some and any		
Statement	**Negative**	**Question**
There's **some** ice cream in the freezer.	We don't have **any** chicken.	Do you have **any** chocolate cake?

*We use *some* for questions with *can* and *could*.
*Can I have **some** water, please?*

A. Complete the sentences with *some* or *any*.

1. There's _____ chocolate ice cream for dessert.
2. We don't have _____ coffee.
3. There's _____ chicken salad for your lunch.
4. Can I have _____ coffee, please?
5. Is there _____ fish?

B. Unscramble the words to write sentences.

1. some coffee/There's/on the table _____ .
2. some/I have/chocolate/Could/ice cream _____ ?
3. have/We/don't/fruit juice/any _____ .
4. fish/we have/any/Do _____ ?
5. eggs/next to/some/the milk/There are _____ .

Conversation

A. Listen to the conversation. What does the customer order?

Waiter:	Good morning.
Customer:	Could I have some <u>coffee</u>, please?
Waiter:	Sure.
Customer:	Do you have any <u>strawberry ice cream</u>?
Waiter:	No, I'm sorry. We don't have <u>strawberry</u>. We only have <u>chocolate</u>.
Customer:	OK, I'll have some <u>chocolate ice cream</u>.

 B. Practice the conversation with a partner. Switch roles and practice it again.

 C. Change the underlined words and make a new conversation.

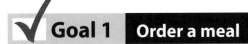
✓ Goal 1   Order a meal

Change partners. Role-play ordering a meal.

Listening

Miguel and Diana are planning a party. Miguel is writing a shopping list.

🎧 **A.** Listen and complete Miguel's shopping list.

Track 2-12

_____ bottles of soda
1 bag of _____
20 _____
10 _____

👥 **B.** Role-play buying the food on Miguel's shopping list.

> Could I have some soda, please?

> How many bottles do you want?

Pronunciation: *And*

A. Listen and check the correct column. Listen and check (✓) the correct column of the form you hear.

	Full form	Short form
1. pasta and salad	✓	
2. pasta and salad		✓
3. fruit juice and cereal		
4. fruit juice and cereal		
5. chocolate cake and ice cream		
6. chocolate cake and ice cream		

 B. Take turns reading the following sentences using the short form.

1. I like hot dogs and hamburgers.
2. Jill and David are good friends.
3. How many brothers and sisters do you have?
4. We have strawberry ice cream and chocolate ice cream.

Communication

Plan a dinner.

1. Decide who to invite.
2. Make a menu for the party.
3. Decide where the guests sit.

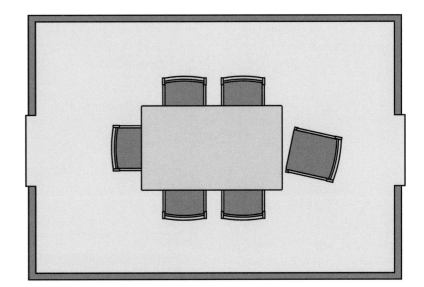

Goal 2   **Plan a party**

Join another group. Explain your menu and table seating.

Language Expansion: Countable and uncountable nouns

The Eatwell Plate

The Eatwell Plate helps you to eat a good diet. It shows the types of food to eat and also how much of each type of food to eat.

A. Write the food in the correct column.

Countable nouns (plural ending -s)	Uncountable nouns
oranges	rice

B. Add the names of other food to the Eatwell Plate. Then list each as a countable or uncountable noun.

Grammar: *How much* and *how many*

How much and *how many*	
Countable nouns	**Uncountable nouns**
How many oranges do you need?	**How much** milk do we have?

How much and how many are used to ask about quantities.

A. Complete the sentences. Use *how much* or *how many*.

1. _____ oranges do you eat every week?
2. _____ candy do you eat?
3. _____ milk do you drink every day?
4. _____ cookies do you eat every day?
5. _____ bread do you eat every day?

 B. Take turns asking and answering the questions in exercise **A** with a partner.

Conversation

A. Listen to the conversation. Does the patient eat well?

Track 2-14

Doctor:	Tell me about the food you eat. How much <u>fruit</u> do you eat?
Patient:	I eat <u>an apple</u> every day. Sometimes I have <u>an orange</u> as well.
Doctor:	Very good! Do you eat <u>meat</u>?
Patient:	Yes, I love <u>meat</u>. I eat a big <u>steak</u> every day.
Doctor:	And <u>vegetables</u>. Do you eat <u>vegetables</u>?
Patient:	No, I don't like <u>vegetables</u>.

 B. Practice the conversation with a partner. Switch roles and practice it again.

 C. Change the underlined words and make a new conversation.

✓ **Goal 3** | **Talk about a healthy diet**

Ask a partner about his/her diet. Is it a healthy diet?

Reading

A. Look at the pictures. Take turns saying which food is ordinary and which food is special.

▲ wedding cake

▲ fried rice

▲ turkey

▲ corn flakes

▲ sandwich

▲ banana flambé

A wedding cake is special food.

B. Answer the questions.

1. When do the Greeks eat *vasilopita*?

   _____

2. How long is the Japanese New Year holiday? _____

3. Why do the Japanese make *Osechi* boxes?

   _____

4. In what country do people eat *Rosca de Reyes*? _____

5. What do people do when they blow out the candles on a birthday cake?

   _____

Word Focus

coin = metal money
doll = a small toy figure like a child

Special Days, Special Food

All over the world, people eat special food on special days. At the New Year in Greece, people eat a special cake called *vasilopita*. Inside the cake, there is a **coin**. They cut the cake, and the person who gets the coin gets good luck.

The Japanese have a three-day holiday at the New Year. They don't like to do any work during the holiday, so they cook the food before it begins. They put the food in boxes called *Osechi* boxes. The food is very beautiful. It is also delicious.

On January 6 in Mexico, people eat a special cake called *Rosca de Reyes*. Inside the cake is a small plastic **doll**. The person who gets the doll has to have a party on February 2 and invite the other people.

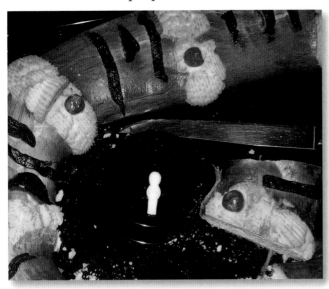

But the best known of all special foods is the birthday cake. All over the world, people celebrate their birthdays with a cake with candles. People blow out the candles and make a wish.

Communication

Answer the questions in the first column. Then ask two classmates the questions.

	Me	Classmate 1	Classmate 2
What do you eat for breakfast?			
How much fruit do you eat each day?			
What do you eat at the New Year?			

Writing

Write about what you eat each day and what you eat on special days.

I usually have eggs for breakfast and a sandwich for lunch. I have dinner at six o'clock. We usually have rice, meat, and vegetables.

At the New Year we eat special noodles, and of course for my birthday I have a birthday cake.

✓ **Goal 4** | **Talk about food for special occasions**

Work with a partner. Make a list of all the special food in your country.

Before You Watch

A. Write the food in the correct column.

hamburger	cheese	fish	mushrooms
pizza	hot dogs	french fries	fruit

▲ cheese

▲ mushrooms

▲ french fries

▲ fruit

▲ pizza

Fast food	Slow food
hamburger	cheese

 B. Tell a partner what foods you like and what foods you don't like.

While You Watch

Answer the questions.

1. Is Greve a big city? _____
2. What three things do the people of Chianti produce? _____
3. Does the mayor want to change Greve? _____
4. What is the goal of the Slow Food Movement? _____
5. What do the farmers of Pistoia produce? _____

After You Watch

A. How can you slow down your life? Label the pictures with the phrases in the box.

spend time with friends and family	take a nap in the afternoon
get more exercise	eat healthy food

B. Discuss with a partner: In what other ways can you slow down your life?

HEALTH

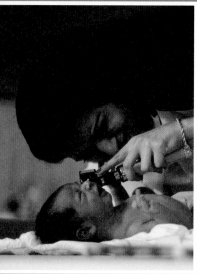

1. Are the people in the pictures healthy?

2. What do you do to stay healthy?

UNIT GOALS

Identify parts of the body to say how you feel
Ask about and describe symptoms
Identify remedies and give advice
Learn and talk about prevention

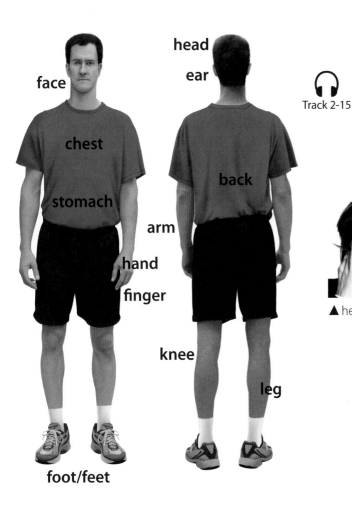

head

ear

face

chest

back

stomach

arm

hand

finger

knee

leg

foot/feet

Vocabulary

🎧
Track 2-15

A. Listen and repeat the parts of the body.

B. How are they feeling? Complete the sentences with words from the box.

terrible   sick   OK   well   great

▲ headache   ▲ fever   ▲ cough

▲ backache   ▲ stomachache

1. John is _____. He has a fever, a cough, and a bad headache.
2. Mary isn't _____. She has a stomachache.
3. Michael is _____. His fever is gone today.
4. Jane feels _____. She isn't sick and today's her birthday.
5. Susan is feeling _____. She has a backache and can't move.

Grammar: *Feel, look*

Statement	Negative	*Yes/no* questions	Information questions
I **feel** sick. He/she **looks** sick.	Hilary **doesn't feel** great. You **don't look** well.	**Do** you **feel** OK? **Does** he/she **look** tired?	How do you feel?
*The verbs *look* and *feel* are followed by an adjective.			

A. Match the sentences with the responses.

1. How do you feel? ____
2. Do you feel OK? ____
3. Does Alan look well? ____
4. How do they feel? ____
5. Sarah doesn't look well. ____

a. No, she isn't feeling well.
b. I feel fine.
c. No, he doesn't. He looks sick.
d. No, I feel terrible.
e. They feel OK.

B. Complete the sentences.

1. **A:** Do you feel OK?
   B: Yes, I _____
2. **A:** How is Melanie?
   B: She doesn't _____ well.
3. **A:** How _____?
   B: I feel terrible.
4. **A:** You don't look very well.
   B: No, I _____.
5. **A:** Does Gerardo look OK?
   B: No, _____ sick.

> **Real Language**
>
> We can ask about someone's health by using the following questions.
>
> Formal ◄————————————► Informal
> *What's the matter?*   *What's wrong?*   *What's up?*
>
> *How are you?* is a greeting. We do not normally use it to ask about someone's health.

Conversation

A. Listen to the conversation. What's wrong with Kim?

Track 2-16

Stephanie: What's the matter, Kim? You don't look well.
Kim: I don't feel well. My <u>head</u> hurts.
Stephanie: Oh, dear!
Kim: And I feel <u>sick</u>.
Stephanie: Maybe you have the flu.

 B. Practice the conversation with a partner. Switch roles and practice it again.

 C. Change the underlined words and make a new conversation.

✓ **Goal 1**   **Identify parts of the body to say how you feel**

Take turns asking a partner how he or she feels today. Be creative with your aches and pains.

Listening

Track 2-17

A. Listen to the conversations. List the patients' symptoms.

Patient 1	Patient 2

B. Look at the pictures. Take turns asking about these people and describing their symptoms.

▲ She has a cold.

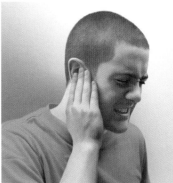

▲ He has an earache.

▲ He has a toothache.

▲ She has a sore throat.

▲ They have measles.

What's the matter with her?

Her throat hurts.

She has a fever.

Pronunciation: Word Stress

A. Listen and notice the stressed syllables.

Track 2-18

Doctor:	How can I <u>help</u> you?
Patient:	I don't feel very <u>well</u>. I have a <u>head</u>ache.
Doctor:	Anything <u>else</u>?
Patient:	Yes, I have a <u>fe</u>ver.
Doctor:	OK. I think I need to ex<u>a</u>mine you.

B. Listen to the conversation. Underline the stressed syllables.

Track 2-19

Dentist:	How are you today?
Patient:	I have a terrible toothache.
Dentist:	Where does it hurt?
Patient:	Right here.
Dentist:	I see the problem.

Communication

Role-play the following situations.

Situation 1

Student A
You are a doctor. Ask your patient how she/he feels.

Student B
You are the patient. You have a cough, a headache, and a fever.

Situation 2

Student B
You are a dentist. Ask your patient how she/he is.

Student A
You are the patient. You have a toothache.

Where does it hurt?

Does it hurt a lot?

✔ Goal 2 Ask about and describe symptoms

Work with a partner. Make a list of ailments. Then take turns describing the symptoms of each one.

Language Expansion: Remedies

▲ go to bed

▲ see a doctor

▲ lie down

▲ see a dentist

▲ take some cough medicine

▲ take some aspirin

Answer the questions. Use the phrases above.

1. What do you do when you have a headache? _____
2. What do you do when you have a backache? _____
3. What do you do when you have a cough? _____
4. What do you do when you have a toothache? _____
5. What do you do when you have a fever? _____

Grammar: *Should* (for advice)

Statement	Negative	*Yes/no* question	*Wh-* question	Short answers
You **should** go to bed. He **should** take some cough medicine.	He **shouldn't** go to work today.	**Should** I see a doctor?	What **should** I do?	Yes, you **should**. No, you **shouldn't**.

*We use *should* to ask for and give advice.

A. Match the questions and the answers.

1. Should I see a doctor? ___
2. I have a headache. What should I do? ___
3. Paul has a toothache. What should he do? ___
4. Should Helen see a doctor? ___
5. Hilary has a cough. What should she do? ___

a. You should take some aspirin.
b. He should see a dentist.
c. She should take some cough medicine.
d. Yes, you should.
e. No, she shouldn't.

 B. Complete the conversations and then practice them with a partner.

1. **A:** I have a headache. What should I do?
   B: _____

2. **A:** I think I have the flu. What should I do?
   B: _____

3. **A:** I have a stomachache. What should I do?
   B: _____

4. **A:** I think my computer has a virus. What should I do?
   B: _____

Conversation

Track 2-20

A. Listen to the conversation. What does Casey think Brenda should do?

Casey: Hi. What's up, Brenda?
Brenda: I don't feel well. I <u>think I have the flu</u>. What should I do?
Casey: I think you should <u>go home and go to bed</u>.
Brenda: Do you think I should see a doctor?
Casey: No, I don't think so.

 B. Practice the conversation with a partner. Switch roles and practice it again.

 C. Change the underlined words and make a new conversation.

 Goal 3 **Identify remedies and give advice**

Work with a partner. Take turns naming an ailment and suggest a remedy or give advice.

I have a toothache.

You should go to the dentist.

Reading

A. Check the things we can prevent. Compare your answer with a partner's answers. How can we prevent them?

- ☐ flu
- ☐ rain
- ☐ toothache
- ☐ headache

Word Focus

prevent = avoid a problem before it happens

infectious disease = a disease you can get from another person

vaccine = medicine to prevent a disease

B. Read the article. Circle **T** for *true* and **F** for *false*.

1.	There is a vaccine for measles.	T	F
2.	About 40,000 children die from malaria every day in Africa.	T	F
3.	There is a vaccine for malaria.	T	F
4.	Mosquito nets are expensive.	T	F
5.	Influenza is a problem in hot countries.	T	F

Preventing Disease

Many people, especially children, die from **infectious diseases** every year. We can **prevent** many infectious diseases. Let's look at the most dangerous ones.

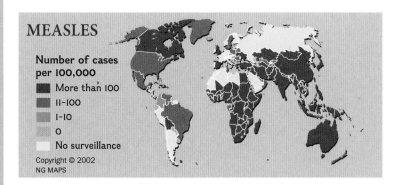

MEASLES

Number of cases
per 100,000
- More than 100
- 11–100
- 1–10
- 0
- No surveillance

Copyright © 2002
NG MAPS

Measles is mainly a children's disease. There is a very good, cheap **vaccine** for measles. All children should get the vaccine but unfortunately not all do. About 900,000 children die every year from measles.

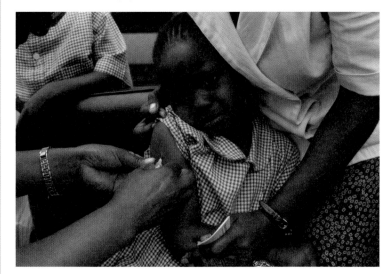

▲ All children should get a measles shot.

MALARIA

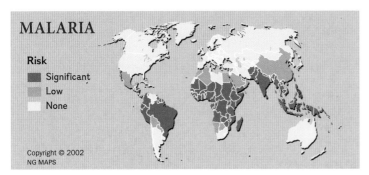

Risk
- ■ Significant
- ■ Low
- □ None

Copyright © 2002
NG MAPS

Imagine seven Jumbo jets full of children. Now, imagine that all the Jumbos crash and all the children are killed. That's how many children die from malaria in Africa *every day*. There is no vaccine for malaria, but it is not difficult to prevent. All you need is a $5 mosquito net.

▲ Children should sleep under a mosquito net.

INFLUENZA (FLU)

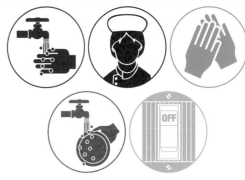

Outbreaks
- ■ Widespread
- ■ Regional
- ■ Local
- ■ Sporadic
- □ Negligible or no surveillance

Copyright © 2002
NG MAPS

Influenza (or flu) is caused by a virus. The virus changes every year so scientists have to make a new vaccine every year. People at risk—for example, older people—should have a flu shot every year. There are good years and bad years. In a bad year, influenza can kill millions of people.

Writing

👥 Complete this notice. Use the words and expressions in the box.

| cover | gloves | switch off | wash your hands | clean |

You should always:

_____ before entering the kitchen.

_____ your hair.

Use oven _____.

Keep the kitchen _____.

_____ electrical equipment.

Communication

👥 Discuss how you can prevent these problems.

| toothache | car accidents |
| heart attacks | computer viruses |

You should brush your teeth.

You shouldn't eat a lot of candy.

You should see a dentist every six months.

✓ **Goal 4** | **Learn and talk about prevention**

Share your best ideas from the communication activity with the class.

Before You Watch

A. Look at the pictures. How dangerous do you think these animals are? Rate them 1 to 4.

▲ lion   ▲ mosquito   ▲ tarantula   ▲ leopard

B. Complete the sentences. Use the words in the box.

| insecticide | repellent | flowers | sun-dried | dry climate |

1. Today's my mother's birthday. I always give her _____.
2. We need mosquito _____ when we go fishing at the lake.
3. This tomato sauce is very good. Does it have _____ tomatoes?
4. It never rains here. We have a very _____.
5. Please buy some _____. There are insects in the house.

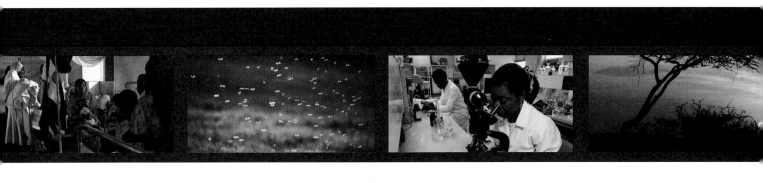

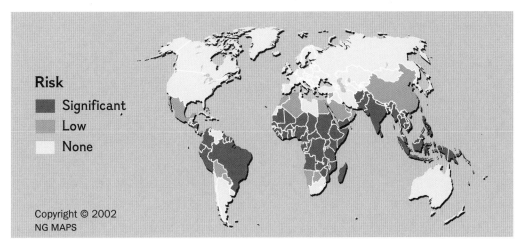

Risk
- Significant
- Low
- None

Copyright © 2002
NG MAPS

While You Watch

 A. Circle **T** for *true* and **F** for *false*. Watch the video again to check your answers.

1.	Pyrethrum flowers attract malaria mosquitoes.	T F
2.	Mosquitoes are resistant to many insecticides.	T F
3.	Doctors make medicine from pyrethrum flowers.	T F
4.	Many children die each year from malaria.	T F
5.	Pyrethrum flowers grow well in dry climates.	T F

 B. Study the map. With a partner locate the countries around the world where malaria is a serious disease.

After You Watch

Discuss other plants and flowers that prevent or cure illnesses. Report to the class.

_____

_____

_____

_____

_____

MAKING PLANS

1. What are your plans for the weekend?

2. What are your plans for your life?

UNIT GOALS

Plan special days
Plan holidays
Make life plans
Express wishes and plans

Vocabulary

▲ go out for dinner

▲ have a party

▲ have a barbeque

▲ go to a club

▲ go to the movies

▲ have a family meal

January 7th, Dad's birthday

February 17th, John's birthday

March

April   1st, Mom and Dad's anniversary

May   14th, My birthday

June   3rd, Mom's birthday

July   24th, Grandpa and Grandma's anniversary

A. Look at the Year Planner and pictures. Decide the best way to celebrate. Complete the sentences.

1. On Dad's birthday, we usually _have a party._
2. On Mom's and Dad's anniversary, they usually _____
3. On John's birthday, we usually _____
4. On Mom's birthday, she usually _____
5. On my birthday, _____
6. On Grandpa and Grandma's anniversary, we _____

> What do you usually do on your birthday?

B. Tell a partner what you usually do on your birthday.

Grammar: *Be going to*

Be going to			
Statement	**Negative**	***Yes/no* question**	***Wh-* question**
I **am going to** have a party.	**We are not going to** have a big meal.	**Are you going to** go to the movies?	What **are you going to** do? When **are we going to** go?

*We use *be going to* for making plans.
*We also use these time expressions: *tomorrow, next Saturday/week/year.*

A. Complete the sentences. Use the words in parentheses and *be going to*.

1. **A:** What _____ (you do) for your birthday?
   B: I _____ have a BIG party!
2. **A:** _____ (you have) a barbeque on the weekend?
   B: No, we _____ (go) to the movies.
3. **A:** Where _____ (Brenda and Alan go) on New Year's?
   B: They _____ go to Times Square.

 B. Practice the conversations with a partner.

Conversation

Track 2-21

A. Listen to the conversation. When is Susan's birthday?

Sally: When is your birthday?
Susan: It's on <u>May 21</u>.
Sally: Hey, that's next week. Are you going to <u>have a party</u>?
Susan: No, I'm going to <u>go out for dinner with my parents</u>.

 B. Practice the conversation with a partner. Switch roles and practice it again.

C. Change the underlined words and make a new conversation.

Goal 1   Plan special days

Take turns asking a partner how he or she celebrates birthdays.

Listening

A. Read about American holidays.

American Holidays

▲ On Thanksgiving Day, people have a family meal.

▲ All over the United States, people celebrate Independence Day with fireworks.

▲ On New Year's in New York, people go to Times Square to celebrate.

▲ At Christmas, people decorate their houses and give presents.

B. Listen and write which holidays the people are talking about.

Track 2-22

Linda and Kenichi are talking about _____.
Tom and Maria are talking about _____.

C. Listen again and answer the questions.

Track 2-22

1. Why isn't Linda going to go to Times Square? _____
2. What is she going to do? _____
3. Where is Kenichi going to go? _____
4. What are Tom and Maria going to do? _____
5. What time is Tom leaving? _____

Pronunciation: *Be going to* (short form)

Track 2-23

A. Listen and check the correct column of the form you hear.

	Full form	Short form
1. We're going to have a party	✓	
2. We're going to have a party		✓
3. I'm going to go to Paris.		
4. I'm going to go to Paris.		
5. They're not going to come.		
6. They're not going to come.		

B. Practice the dialogs with a partner. Use the short form of *be going to*.

A: What are you going to do on the weekend?
B: I'm going to go to the beach.

A: Are you going to go to Kim's party?
B: No, I'm going to stay home this weekend.

Communication

Write a list of holidays in your country. Discuss what you are going to do on *those* days.

✓ **Goal 2**   **Plan holidays**

Join another pair of students and tell them
about two holidays on your list.

Language Expansion: Professions

▲ law

▲ nursing

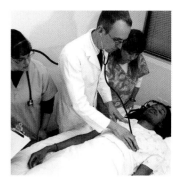
▲ medicine

▲ music

▲ acting

▲ psychology

Match the person to the profession.

1. doctor _____   a. music
2. lawyer _____   b. medicine
3. musician _____   c. psychology
4. nurse _____   d. acting
5. actor _____   e. law
6. psychologist _____ f. nursing

Grammar: *Would like to* for wishes

Statement	Yes/no question	Short answer	*Wh-* question
I **would like to** be a doctor. Danny **would like to** study law.	**Would** you **like to** study engineering? **Would** you **like to** be a nurse?	Yes, I **would**. No, I **wouldn't**.	What **would** you **like to** be?

A. Unscramble the words to write sentences.

1. to be a would like I musician. _____
2. Eleanor like What would to be? _____
3. to be Would you a doctor? like _____
4. Deng nursing. would to study like _____
5. What like to be? would you _____

B. Write the wishes or plans.

Wish	Plan
1. *I would like to be an actor.*	I am going to be an actor.
2. Danny would like to study medicine.	_____
3. _____	I am going to be a doctor.
4. We would like to leave at seven o'clock.	_____
5. _____	They are going to study nursing.

Conversation

Track 2-24

A. Listen to the conversation. What would Wendy like to be?

Father: So, Wendy, you're 18 years old today. What are you going to do with your life?

Wendy: Well, I'd like to get married and have children.

Father: Whoa! Not so quick!

Wendy: Only joking! I'd like to be a <u>lawyer</u>. I'd like to study <u>law</u> and become a <u>lawyer</u>.

 B. Practice the conversation with a partner. Switch roles and practice it again.

 C. Change the underlined words and make a new conversation.

Real Language

We can say *Only joking* to show we are not serious.

Goal 3 Make life plans

Talk to a partner. What would you like to do with your life?

Reading

A. Look at the pictures. Where do you think these people come from? Read and check your guesses.

B. Read and answer the questions.

1. How old is Annalien? _____
2. What would she like to be? _____
3. Where would she like to study?
   _____
4. Why is today Zanelle's big day?
   _____
5. Does Zanelle have children? _____
6. What are Vasili and Olga celebrating?
   _____
7. What are they going to do?
   _____

C. Check (✔) the correct box.

	Wish	Plan
1. Annalien: I would like to study acting.	☐	☐
2. Zanelle is going to get married.	☐	☐
3. Zanelle would like to have a lot of children.	☐	☐
4. Vasili and Olga are going to dance all night.	☐	☐

Life's Milestones

In some Central American and Caribbean countries, a girl's 15th birthday is very important.

Here, Elsa Mendoza prepares her niece, Annalien, for her 15th-birthday photographs.

Annalien would like to study acting in Havana. Her aunt told her that she has to finish school first. "She's not ready to go to the big city yet."

Zanelle is an Ndebele from South Africa. Today is her big day. She is going to get married. However, she is not truly married until she has her first child. She says, "I would like to have a lot of children. But most of all, I would like to be happy."

This is Vasili and Olga Karezin. They are from the Ukraine. Today is their golden wedding anniversary. They got married 50 years ago. What are they going to do on this special day? They are going to have a meal with their family and friends. And then they are going to dance—all night.

Writing

Write a wish and a plan.

I would like to visit Europe. So, I am
going to learn English and I am going
to save some money.

_____

_____

_____

_____

✔ **Goal 4** | **Express wishes and plans**

Share your wishes and plans with a partner.

What would you like to do with your life?

How are you going to do it?

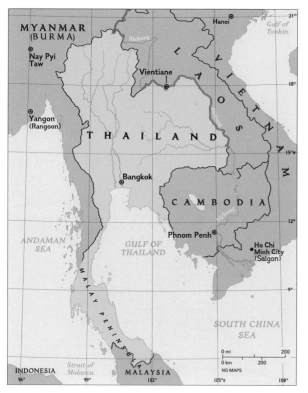

Before You Watch

A. Read about the video. With a partner try to guess the meanings of the words in bold.

> ### Video Summary
>
> Thai **boxing,** or Muay Thai, is a traditional **martial art** from Thailand. Thai boxers use their hands, heads, and legs. Manat is a 12-year-old boy from a poor family who is living at a Thai boxing **training camp**. He trains seven hours a day, seven days a week. He wishes to become a boxing champion. He works very hard.

B. What martial arts do you know? Make a list.

_____

_____

_____

_____

_____

_____

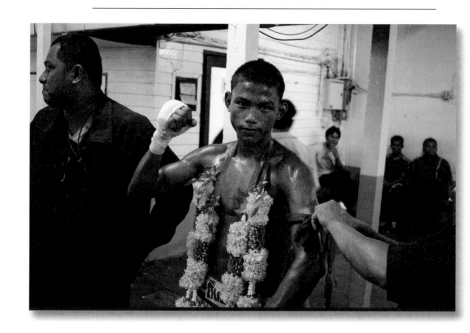

While You Watch

 A. Watch the video. Order the things that you see.

___ Manat doesn't win.
___ Manat goes into the ring for a ceremony.
___ The fight begins.
___ Manat trains very hard.
___ Manat will become a champion.

 B. Watch the video again. Complete the sentences with words from the box.

| family   champion   poor   trains   win |

1. Manat comes from a _____ family.
2. Manat's coaches believe he will be a _____.
3. When Manat wins, he wants to send the money to his _____.
4. Manat doesn't _____.
5. Manat _____ very hard.

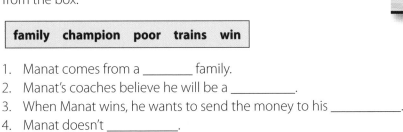

After You Watch

 Answer these questions with a partner.

1. Do you think Manat will get his wish to become a Thai boxing champion?
2. What do you think about the training camp? Name positive and negative things.

MIGRATIONS

1. Why do people move from one country to another?

2. Why do animals move from one place to another?

UNIT GOALS

Talk about moving in the past
Talk about moving dates
Talk about preparations for moving
Discuss migrations

Vocabulary

▲ leave

▲ arrive in/at

▲ return to/from

▲ go to

▲ come from/to

▲ move from/to

▲ stay in/at

Circle the correct verb in parentheses.

1. People (move/leave) their homes when they go to work.
2. They are going to (arrive/come) from Paris tomorrow.
3. I am going to (come/stay) at Jim's house tonight.
4. At the moment, John is (staying/returning) in Toronto.
5. Children (go/stay) to school at eight o'clock.

Grammar: Simple past tense

Simple past tense		
Statement	Negative	*Wh-* questions
He **moved** from New York to San Francisco.	I **didn't stay** in California.	When **did they leave** Germany? How long **did you stay** in France?

*We use the simple past tense to talk about completed actions or conditions.

*Some verbs are regular in the simple past. They have an *-ed* ending.				*Some verbs are irregular in the simple past. They have many different forms.	
return	returned	move	moved	go	went
stay	stayed	live	lived	come	came
arrive	arrived			leave	left

A. Match the questions and the answers.

1. When did you move to Oman? _____
2. How long did you stay in Taipei? _____
3. When did Michelle come to Chile? _____
4. When did Al and Lorena leave Argentina? _____
5. How long did George live in Texas? _____

a. He lived there for eight years.
b. She came in 2008.
c. They left in 2002.
d. I moved there in 2007.
e. I stayed there for two years.

B. Complete the questions and answers.

1. **A:** When did you leave Canada?
   B: I _____ in 2000.
2. **A:** How long _____ in Saudi Arabia?
   B: I stayed there for three years.
3. **A:** Where did you live in Brazil?
   B: We _____ in São Paulo.
4. **A:** When did you arrive in the United States?
   B: I _____ three years ago.

 C. Practice the questions and answers in exercise **B** with a partner.

Conversation

 A. Listen to the conversation. When did Fatima arrive in Canada?

Track 2-25

Ed:	<u>Fatima</u>, you're not <u>Canadian</u>. Do you mind if I ask where you're from?
Fatima:	Well, I was born in <u>Syria</u>, but later my parents moved to <u>France</u>.
Ed:	How long did you stay in <u>France</u>?
Fatima:	Twelve years. But then I left <u>France</u> when I was 18 to study in the <u>United States</u>.
Ed:	And when did you come to <u>Canada</u>?
Fatima:	I came here five years ago.

 B. Practice the conversation. Switch roles and practice it again.

 C. Change the underlined words and make a new conversation.

✓ **Goal 1**   **Talk about moving in the past**

With a partner trace two or three moves that you made (or wanted to make). Make notes of the names of the places. Take turns asking each other about your moves.

Listening

 Track 2-26

A. Do you know these people? Write the name under the photos. Listen and check.

| Albert Einstein   Jerry Yang   Salma Hayek   Anna Kournikova |

Famous immigrants to the United States

Word Focus

We say years like this:

1980 = nineteen eighty
2000 = two thousand
2009 = two thousand nine

1. _____

2. _____

3. _____   4. _____

 Track 2-26

B. Listen carefully for the dates. Circle **T** for *true* and **F** for *false*.

1. Albert Einstein moved to the United States in 1933.   T   F
2. Salma Hayek was born in 1976.   T   F
3. Jerry Yang moved to San Jose in 1976.   T   F
4. Anna Kournikova moved to the United States in 1990.   T   F

Track 2-26

C. Listen again and answer the questions.

1. Where did Albert Einstein go to school? _____
2. Who did Salma Hayek live with in the United States? _____
3. Where did Jerry Yang move to in the United States? _____
4. When did Anna Kournikova start to play tennis? _____

Pronunciation: -ed endings

Track 2-27

A. Listen and check the correct column.

B. Practice these sentences with a partner.

1. He moved to Peru in 1989.
2. They wanted to go to Egypt.
3. My mother cooked a delicious meal.
4. We walked to the beach.
5. I traveled from Buenos Aires by plane.
6. Kris wanted to buy a new coat.

	/d/ ending	/t/ ending	/ɪd/ ending
1. returned			
2. moved			
3. wanted			
4. traveled			
5. cooked			
6. stayed			
7. lived			
8. walked			

Communication

 Look at the arrows on the map. Take turns asking where and when Alonso and Trudy went. The map shows where. You add the dates.

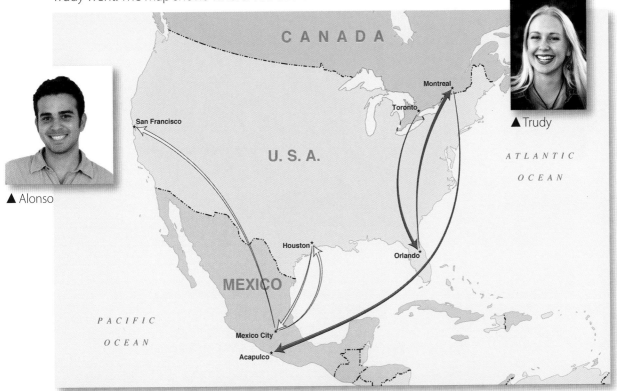

▲ Trudy

▲ Alonso

When did Alonso leave Mexico City?

Where did he go?

✓ **Goal 2**   **Talk about moving dates**

Think of a friend or family member that has moved a lot in the past. Tell a partner where and when he or she moved.

Language Expansion: Preparing to move

Word Focus

Note the following irregular past tenses:

sell—sold   buy—bought
get—got   have—had

▲ sell the house

▲ buy the tickets

▲ pack

▲ get a passport

▲ sell the car

▲ close the bank account

▲ have a farewell party

Write sentences from the checklist.

- ☑ buy the tickets
- ☐ sell the house
- ☑ sell the car
- ☐ get the passports
- ☑ close the bank account

1. *We bought the tickets.*
2. _____
3. _____
4. _____
5. _____

Grammar: Simple past tense

Simple past tense	
Yes/no questions	Short answers
Did they **return** to New York?	Yes, they **did**. No, they **didn't**.

A. Unscramble the words to write questions.

1. farewell / party / have a / Did / they _____ ?
2. you / the / sell / house / Did _____ ?
3. Did / the / tickets / Ian / buy _____ ?
4. close / the / Did / we / windows _____ ?
5. pack / they / their / Did / things _____ ?

B. Complete the sentences. Practice them with a partner.

1. **A:** _____ buy the tickets?
   B: Yes, I _____.

2. **A:** Did you _____?
   B: No, I _____.

3. **A:** Did they _____ the house?
   B: No, _____.

Conversation

A. Where are David and Liana moving? Listen to the conversation.

Track 2-28

David: Did you <u>get the tickets</u>?
Liana: Yes, I did. Here they are.
David: Great!
Liana: And did you <u>sell the car</u>?
David: Yes, I did. I got <u>$3,000</u> for it.
Liana: Wow! Now I can buy some nice warm clothes for Canada.

 B. Practice the conversation. Switch roles and practice it again.

 C. Change the underlined words and make a new conversation.

✓ **Goal 3** **Talk about preparations for moving**

You are going to Australia to study English for the summer. Make plans with a partner. Write a checklist.

Reading

A. At some time in the past, your ancestors moved to your country. Maybe it was 100 years ago; maybe it was 100,000 years ago. Look at the map. Where did they come from?

B. Read and underline the regular verbs and circle the irregular verbs in the simple past tense.

C. Answer the questions.

1. Where did humans first appear?
   _____

2. Where did they migrate to first?
   _____

3. How did people move across the United States? _____

4. Give an example of economic migration.
   _____

5. Give an example of forced migration.
   _____

Word Focus

migrate = to move from one place to another
economic = about money
forced = when something is not what you want
war = a fight

Human Migration

We think that modern humans appeared in Africa about 200,000 years ago. But they didn't stay in Africa. They migrated out of Africa to the Middle East and then to the rest of the world. Throughout history, people have **migrated** from one place to another. People, it seems, like to move.

▲ People moved from the East Coast of the United States to the West Coast in wagon trains.

Since the 17th century, many European people have moved from Europe to the Americas. They left Spain and Portugal and moved to South America. Many Northern Europeans migrated to North America. In the United States, most people arrived in New York. Some stayed on the East Coast, but many people migrated to the West Coast.

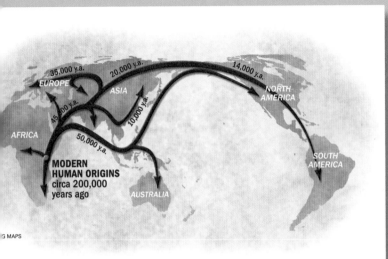

MODERN HUMAN ORIGINS circa 200,000 years ago

G MAPS

So, why do people move? First, there is **economic** migration. People move to find work and a good life. Second, there is **forced** migration. People move because of **wars**; it is not safe to stay in their homes.

▲ These people are from the Congo, in Africa. They left their homes during the war, but now they are returning.

Of course, many people don't migrate. They stay in the same place all their lives. But people like to visit different countries on their vacations. People, it seems, just like to move.

Writing

Read the brochure and write a holiday postcard.

European Three Capital Tour

June 15th	Leave home.
June 16th	Arrive in London. The Tower of London
June 18th	London to Paris. Eiffel Tower, The Louvre
June 20th	Paris to Rome. The Coliseum
June 22nd	Rome to London.
June 23rd	London to home.

We left home on the 15th and arrived in London on the 16th. We visited

_____

_____

_____

_____

_____

Communication

Where would you like to migrate to? Why would you like to live there? Explain to a partner and then to the class.

Goal 4 | **Discuss migrations**

Animals also migrate. What animals migrate? Where do they migrate to and from? Why do they migrate?

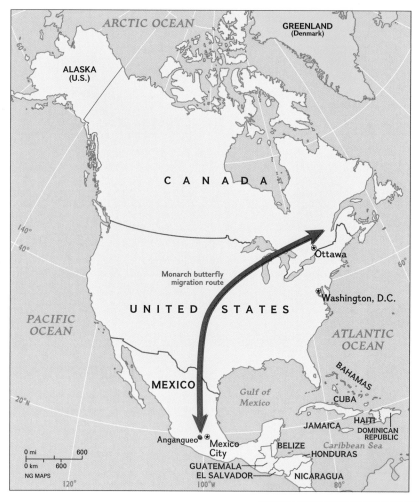

Before You Watch

A. Complete the sentences with words from the box. Use your dictionary.

spectacle	forest	fragile	environment
disaster	logging	destroy	preserve

1. Monarch butterflies are very _____. Cold temperatures can kill them.
2. The monarch migration is very beautiful. It is a _____.
3. Monarch butterflies migrate to a _____ in Mexico.
4. _____, cutting down trees, is going to _____ the forest.
5. Governments and organizations want to _____ the forest.
6. Millions of monarchs will die without their natural _____. It will be a _____.

B. Write each of the words in the box in the correct column.

Positive meaning (+)	Negative meaning (−)	Neutral meaning

While You Watch

A. Watch the video. Match to complete the sentences.

1. Monarch butterflies ___
2. Monarch Watch __
3. Loggers ___
4. The Mexican government ___

    a. pays the landowners $18 per cubic meter of wood they do not cut down.
    b. work at the University of Kansas and observe the butterfly migration.
    c. travel more than 2,000 miles every year.
    d. cut down the trees and destroy the forest.

B. Watch the video again. Write the numbers you hear.

1. More than _____ million monarch butterflies migrate each year.
2. The butterflies travel _____ miles from northern America and Canada to a Mexican forest.
3. In January 2002, a rainstorm and freezing temperatures killed ____ million butterflies.
4. Almost _____ percent of the population in the *El Rosario* butterfly sanctuary died from the cold.
5. There are _____ butterfly sanctuaries in Mexico.
6. In the last _____ years, logging destroyed nearly half the forests the monarchs need.

After you Watch

Discuss the problems of the Monarch migration in your group. Write a list of things that people can do to save these butterflies.

Communication

With a partner think of an animal or plant that has a similar problem in your country or region. Answer these questions:

1. What is the animal or plant?
2. What problem does it have?
3. How can this animal or plant be saved?

Activity 1
Units 1 & 2

 Take turns asking and answering the questions.

   a.   Where is the Brown family from?

   b.   Is it hot or cold in their country?

   c.   What is Mr. Brown's job?

   d.   Are they young or old?

   e.   Is Mr. Brown handsome?

   f.   Are the children pretty?

▲ the Brown family

Real Language

We use *I think . . .* or *Maybe . . .*
when we are not sure about
an answer.

I think they are from Canada.

Maybe they are from Canada.

Activity 2
Units 3 & 4

 Take turns answering the questions.

   a.   What furniture can you see in the house?

   b.   Where is the furniture?

   c.   What electronic products can you see?

   d.   Where are they?

   e.   What personal possessions can you see?

   f.   Where are they?

Activity 3
Units 5 & 6

 Imagine a person who lives in this city. Think about these questions, then tell a partner about that person.

    a. What is the person's name?

    b. Where does the person live?

    c. Where does the person work?

    d. How does he/she get to work?

    e. What route does he/she take?

    f. What does he/she do at work?

    g. What does the person do when he/she gets home from work?

Activity 4
Units 7 & 8

Take turns asking and answering the questions.

    a. What are these people doing?

    b. What are they wearing?

    c. What color are their clothes?

Activity 5
Units 9 & 10

What is a healthy diet? Take turns asking and answering questions like these:

a. Should you eat _____?

b. How much _____ should you eat every day?

Activity 6
Units 11 & 12

Deluxe World Tour
The Tour of a Lifetime

▲ Eiffel Tower
June 20 Paris, France

▲ The Pyramids
June 22 Egypt

▲ Wildebeest migration
June 25 Kenya

▲ the Taj Mahal
June 28 India

▲ the Great Wall
July 1 China

▲ Disneyland
July 3 Los Angeles, California, USA

STUDENT A

You are going to go on this tour. Student B took this tour last year. Ask questions like:

  a. Where did you go?

  b. When did you arrive in _____?

  c. How long did you stay in _____?

  d. What did you do in _____?

STUDENT B

You went on the tour last year. Student A is taking the tour this year. Ask questions like:

  a. Where are you going to go?

  b. How long are you staying in _____?

  c. What are you going to do in _____?

SKILLS INDEX

CREDITS

ILLUSTRATION

iv-v: National Geographic Maps; **6:** Ted Hammond/IllustrationOnline.com; **7:** Nesbitt Graphics, Inc.; **8:** Ted Hammond/IllustrationOnline.com; **11, 12, 20, 22, 23:** National Geographic Maps; **24, 25:** (all) Bob Kayganich/IllustrationOnline.com; **28:** (both) Patrick Gnan/IllustrationOnline.com; **29:** Nesbitt Graphics, Inc.; **32, 33, 35:** (all) Patrick Gnan/IllustrationOnline.com; **36:** (t) Mapping Specialists, Ltd. Madison, WI, USA, (br) Bob Kayganich/IllustrationOnline.com; **40:** Bob Kayganich/IllustrationOnline.com; **44, 52, 54:** Nesbitt Graphics, Inc.; **60:** National Geographic Maps; **64, 65:** Bob Kayganich/IllustrationOnline.com; **66:** National Geographic Maps; **68:** Nesbitt Graphics, Inc.; **70:** National Geographic Maps; **72:** (l) Mapping Specialists, Ltd. Madison, WI, USA, (r) Bob Kayganich/IllustrationOnline.com; **78:** Keith Neely/IllustrationOnline.com; **85:** National Geographic Maps; **88:** (t) Nesbitt Graphics, Inc., (b) Keith Neely/IllustrationOnline.com; **92:** Nesbitt Graphics, Inc; **96:** National Geographic Maps; **102, 103, 104:** Bob Kayganich/IllustrationOnline.com; **112, 114:** Ralph Voltz/IllustrationOnline.com; **118, 119, 121:** National Geographic Maps; **119, 124:** Nesbitt Graphics, Inc.; **132:** National Geographic Maps; **136:** Ted Hammond/IllustrationOnline.com; **139:** Patrick Gnan/IllustrationOnline.com; **143, 144:** National Geographic Maps.

PHOTO

Cover photo: Remi Benali/Corbis.

iv: (tl) PhotostoGo.com, (mr) Gail Johnson/Shutterstock, (b) Charles Shapiro/Shutterstock; **v:** (tl) Kheng Guan Toh/Shutterstock, (tr) Upperhall/JupiterImages, (m) Steve Silver/AGE Fotostock, (b) David Reed/AGE Fotostock; **2–3:** (l to r) Annie Griffiths Belt/National Geographic Image Collection, Winfield Parks/National Geographic Image Collection, Ira Block/National Geographic Image Collection, Steve Winter/National Geographic Image Collection; **4:** (tl) photos.com, (tr) Sharon Dominick /iStockphoto, (tr, background) Rade Kovac/Shutterstock, (bl) Jacob Wackerhausen/iStockphoto, (br) BananaStock/JupiterImages; **6:** (l) Aldo Murillo/iStockphoto, (m) Blend Images/JupiterImages, (r) Jennifer Zolzer/iStockphoto; **8:** (top, l to r) iStockphoto (2), Stephanie Phillips/iStockphoto, PhotostoGo.com, (middle, t to b) iStockphoto, Shelly Perry/iStockphoto, iStockphoto, Pete Collins/iStockphoto; **9:** (t) AVAVA/Shutterstock, (b) Kevin Russ/iStockphoto; **10:** (t) Joey Nelson/iStockphoto, (b) Michael S. Yamashita/National Geographic Image Collection; **11:** (l) Kris Leboutillier/National Geographic Image Collection, (right, clockwise from tl) Jacob Wackerhausen/iStockphoto, Kevin Russ/iStockphoto, Oleg Dubas/Shutterstock, Carmen Martínez Banús/iStockphoto; **12–13:** (l to r) Dan Westergren/National Geographic Image Collection, Joel Sartore/National Geographic Image Collection, Maria Stenzel/National Geographic Image Collection, Clickit/Shutterstock, George F. Mobley/National Geographic Image Collection, Frans Lanting/National Geographic Image Collection, Clickit/Shutterstock, Dan Westergren/National Geographic Image Collection; **12:** (1) Michael Nichols/National Geographic Image Collection, (2) Nico Smit/iStockphoto, (3) Joel Sartore/National Geographic Image Collection, (4) photos.com, (5) Chris Johns/National Geographic Image Collection, (6) Nico Smit/iStockphoto; **13:** (bottom, l to r) Chris Johns/National Geographic Image Collection, Tubuceo/Shutterstock, iStockphoto, Joel Sartore/National Geographic Image Collection, John Pitcher/iStockphoto; **14–15:** (l to r) Charles O'Rear/National Geographic Image Collection, Tino Soriano/National Geographic Image Collection, Xinhua /Landov, George F. Mobley/National Geographic Image Collection; **16:** (1) PhotostoGo.com, (2) H. Edward Kim/National Geographic Image Collection, (3) Carrie Bottomley/iStockphoto, (4) Theo Westenberger/National Geographic Image Collection, (5) Comstock Images/JupiterImages, (6) Jose Manuel Gelpi Diaz/iStockphoto, (7) Andrew Lever/Shutterstock, (8) iStockphoto; **17:** PhotostoGo.com; **18:** (l) Bonnie Jacobs/iStockphoto, (m) Wilson Valentin/iStockphoto, (r) Diego Cervo/Shutterstock; **19:** Andrea Gingerich/iStockphoto; **20:** (l to r) Lars Christensen/iStockphoto, Giorgio Fochesato/iStockphoto, Vladimirs Koskins/Shutterstock, Surkov Vladimir/Shutterstock; **21:** Digital Vision/Getty Images; **22:** James L. Amos/National Geographic Image Collection; **23:** (top, l to r) Tish1/Shutterstock, Yali Shi/iStockphoto, John Scofield/National Geographic Image Collection, JupiterImages/Getty Images, (b) W. Robert Moore/National Geographic Image Collection; **24–25:** (l to r) Franziska Lang/Shutterstock, Rita Januskeviciute/Shutterstock, Josep Pique Alecha/iStockphoto, Gail Johnson/Shutterstock, Sophie Demange/iStockphoto, Chris Pole/Shutterstock, Gail Johnson/Shutterstock, Sophie Demange/iStockphoto; **24:** (b) Sophie Demange/iStockphoto; **25:** (b) Robert S. Patton/National Geographic Image Collection; **26–27:** (l to r) Justin Guariglia/National Geographic Image Collection, Michael Shake/Shutterstock, PhotostoGo.com, Ed Kashi/National Geographic Image Collection; **29:** Justin Horrocks/iStockphoto; **30:** (tl) Keisuke Iwamoto/Sebun Photo/Getty Images, (tr) Steve Lovegrove/iStockphoto, (ml) RCPPHOTO/Shutterstock, (mr) David Hughes/Shutterstock, (b) Rohit Seth/Shutterstock; **31:** (l) Thierry Maffeis/Shutterstock, (r) Mike J. Roberts/Shutterstock; **32:** (top, l to r) Stephanie Phillips/iStockphoto, Maksym Bondarchuk/iStockphoto, James Phelps/iStockphoto, Geoffrey Holman/iStockphoto, (middle, l to r) Lars Christensen/iStockphoto, Simon Krži/iStockphoto, Bonita Hein/iStockphoto, trailexplorers/Shutterstock, (bottom, l to r) Dmitry Kutlayev/iStockphoto, Arthur Fatykhov/iStockphoto, Margo Harrison/Shutterstock, White Smoke/Shutterstock; **33:** (top, l to r) Joy Brown/Shutterstock, Juriah Mosin/Shutterstock, photos.com, Harry Hu/Shutterstock, Ryan McVay/AGE Fotostock, (bl) Chris Rodenberg Photography/Shutterstock, (br) PhotostoGo.com; **34:** (l) George Steinmetz Photography, (tr) George Steinmetz/National Geographic Image Collection, (br) Norbert Rosing/National Geographic Image Collection; **35:** (t) Photodisc/Getty Images, (b) Tomasz Broszkiewicz; **36–37:** (l to r) PhotostoGo.com, Seet/Shutterstock, Massimo Bassano/National Geographic Image Collection, Antonio S./Shutterstock, PhotostoGo.com, Lucio Pompeo/iStockphoto, Antonio S./Shutterstock, Massimo Bassano/National Geographic Image Collection;